Thanks for the Memories

Thanks for the Memories

More Stories from Calgary's Past
by Jack Peach

FIFTH HOUSE
PUBLISHERS

Front cover photographs courtesy Glenbow-Alberta Institute (Streetcar: NA-1299-2; CPR messengers: ND-3-2322; Fire station: NA-967-3) and Provincial Archives of Alberta (Oil drillers: P. 1303). Photograph of Jack Peach courtesy Audrey Peach.

Cover design by NEXT Communications Inc.

The publisher gratefully acknowledges the support received from The Canada Council, Heritage Canada, and the Saskatchewan Arts Board. Special thanks to Audrey Peach for her cooperation and to Lynette Walton of the Glenbow-Alberta Institute for her assistance with the photographs.

Printed and bound in Canada by Best Gagné Book Manufacturers
94 95 96 97 98 / 5 4 3 2 1

CANADIAN CATALOGUING IN PUBLICATION DATA

Peach, Jack

Thanks for the memories

ISBN 1-895618-50-9

1. Calgary (Alta.) - History. 2. Calgary (Alta.) - Biography. I. Title.

FC3697.4.P424 1994 971.23'38 C94-920095-6
F1079.5.C35P424 1994

Note: The author used both imperial and metric systems in his columns. Those imperial measurements necessary to the historical context of the material have not been converted.

Fifth House Ltd.
620 Duchess Street
Saskatoon, SK, Canada
S7K 0R1

Contents

What Are Little Boys Made Of?

*T*ALK ABOUT YOUR MODERN HANGUPS OF SEXual discrimination and equal opportunity! During my childhood, girls gleefully chanted the poem:

> What are little girls made of?
> Sugar and spice and all things nice.
> That's what little girls are made of!
> And what are little boys made of?
> Snakes and snails and puppy dogs' tails.
> That's what little boys are made of!

That was sexist and false. So, chauvinists, here is the true story of what little boys were made of.

One of the most distinctive things about a little boy was his pocket watch. Mine was an Ingersoll that cost my father one dollar. There was a whole card of dollar watches standing on the glass-topped counter of every United Cigar Store, each housed in a sturdy nickel-plated case. Some even had black faces and luminous numbers and hands.

For some reason the older kids called them "turnips." The big, honest, open-faced timepieces had a knurled winder within a ring above the number "12" and a ratchet that sounded like a ship's windlass. You found a chain or a leather thong and, if possible, a fob. My watch was white metal, the size of a fifty-cent piece, had a bit of blue enamel, and a likeness of a smiling planet and some stars. That's because it advertised Marr's Plumbing Limited of Calgary.

When a kid asked you what time it was, you'd fish it out, gaze lovingly into its bland face, and pompously announce, "Well, I make 'er exactly twelve to three." Having thus declared all was well with the world, you'd return the turnip to the dark safety of a special pocket high at the top right-hand front of your trousers.

Occasionally the Ingersoll needed adjusting, not because of shock or wear, but because of the season or altitude or some other equally divine intervention. Adjusting the watch was a job for your father. With the sharp edge of his pocket knife blade he would snap off the back, laying bare the innermost secrets of the Ingersoll's anatomy.

While he adjusted the speed with a knife-tip, he'd let you peer into the hefty cogs and plates, as long as you held your breath to "keep dampness from the machinery." Was that watch wear-proof, child-proof, shock-proof? Well, can a ten year old bend a tractor? Of course not! Neither could he break the spirit of an Ingersoll nickel-plated dollar watch. That's one of the things little boys were made of.

Another was the pocket knife. You could hardly wait until you were old enough to be given one for Christmas. Those were the days when only wicked men in far-off places used a knife dangerously. Yours was for digging out slivers, sharpening pencils, cutting apple cores, whittling when time hung heavily, slicing matchsticks into toothpicks,

Jack and his sister, Mary, holding pennant after winning sandcastle competition at Sylvan Lake.
Courtesy Glenbow-Alberta Institute/NA-2139-1

and chipping mud off your shoes or the valve covers of your bicycle tires.

The pocket knife you dreamed of had a staghorn handle encasing a main blade and one smaller blade. In time you graduated to the Official Scout Knife you were entitled to order by mail as soon as you reached the age of twelve. It had three blades, a corkscrew, awl, nail file, and a sort of digger-outer of everything.

If ever you lost or misplaced your knife you were left a whimpering cripple, even though opening the blades usually cost a fingernail.

Still no snakes and snails and puppy dogs' tails.

Instead there were cats' eyes and alleys and agates and dibs found in a bag of about fifty marbles that every boy carried in his already laden pockets. The brightly coloured glazed clay dibs predominated. Woolworth's on Eighth Avenue—next to the Royal Bank near Centre Street—would sell you fifty for a nickel.

You won and lost with the panache of a Mississippi riverboat gambler, picking up not only the marbleise lingo but also a splendid assortment of glass agates: swirly white milkies and the rare and prized blueys. Trading marbles was a thriving schoolyard business, and the blueys were the gold sovereigns of a marble player's currency.

Even more precious were the ballbarians. Any worthy Calgary marbler knew that was the only pronunciation. If you said otherwise you were obviously an outsider, a foreigner—perhaps from as far away as Manitoba. We would prowl through garages such as Tim Horne's on Seventeenth Avenue at 26A Street West in hopes of finding a steely.

Speaking of pronunciations, we Calgary juvenile marble players scoffed at outsiders—such as kids from Victoria—who said, "I bags that one" when they claimed possession of a forfeited marble. Saskatchewan kids were even worse with their "I fair that one." How ignorant could you get when anyone of any intelligence knew it was "I bonies that one."

The fourth element in a boy's make-up in the Calgary of the 1920s was his top, which was as much a part of springtime as the first robin. It was made of solid hardwood, turnip-shaped, with a metal cone at the pointy end. You held the top in your left hand, point up, and wound a strong linen cord tightly until you reached the big flat top of the top. (Sorry about that!)

You then changed hands because the string had a loop at the end through which you put your right forefinger. Then, with a sharp flick of your wrist, you flung the top at the ground, whipping your hand back in the same motion. The top, suddenly free of the string, would spin like mad until it lost momentum and circled, as though wounded, then lay still. Each spring there was a brisk trade in tops; colour and size somehow having a magical bearing on performance. Becoming the school's top-spinning champion was a distinct honour.

All right, you sexists, now you know, really and truly:

Turnips and blades
and agates and trades.
That's what little boys were made of!

High Water Adventures

CALGARY WOULD NOT BE THE SAME WITHOUT the Bow and the Elbow rivers. The Bow got off to an especially bad start at the hands of the white men, who used it as a convenient and reliable sewer. The town's main effluent outlet was at the river's south bank at the foot of today's First Street East. There were a few smaller deliberate spills from factories downstream, and, with little remorse or improvement, the disgusting practice survived until 1932, by which time Calgary had a population of over eighty thousand.

One of the first recorded Elbow River adventures took place in 1883. Pioneer settler Felix Alexander McHugh had a contract with the Fort Calgary mounted police to cut timber for fencing and fortifications along the Elbow thirty-two kilometres upstream from the fort. Winter overtook the project and in the warmth of spring the logs broke free of the ice and collided with the CPR bridge near the river's mouth.

For the better part of a century, the Elbow River has supplied Calgary with water. It was first tapped for this purpose because public wells placed about the city were inadequate, inconvenient, and unsanitary. In 1907 an eighteen-kilometre wooden stave pipe, seventy-five centimetres in diameter, brought water to Calgary from a location upstream from the Twin Bridges in Springbank. This gravity system took advantage of a ninety-metre drop in altitude between the source and the city. Two years later, the flow of over 30 million litres a day ruptured, and Calgarians had to revert temporarily to the old wells' murky water.

The water system was updated from time to time, and water surge towers and reservoirs were added, but by July 1930 it had become inadequate. Fortunately, at this time, construction of the Glenmore Dam began. The dam not only tamed the Elbow River just in time, but it also created a lake; Calgary had taken a giant step toward year-round water supply.

Only weeks before the Glenmore Dam was completed in the summer of 1932, the Elbow worked itself into a frenzy thanks to a rare combination of high temperature and heavy rain. Luckily that crisis arose just before the freshly logged valley basin had completely filled. Two days later water rose to the lip of the nearly finished dam!

In those days the Elbow could become a brawling torrent when well fed by mountain waters. Now we drink about two-thirds of it, making it an entirely different stream. It regularly and unmercifully teased parts of Calgary by surging over its banks in springtime, silting low-lying places, and making residential and business life along its otherwise picturesque banks a soggy and hazardous undertaking. One of our annual escapes from classes at Western Canada High consisted of launching our homemade puntlike boats to help the post, milk, grocery, and bakery delivery men

The Bow and Elbow rivers have been the source of both pleasure and heartache over the years. In 1915 the Bow River played havoc with the Centre Street Bridge. *Courtesy Glenbow-Alberta Institute/NA-4355-13*

make (dry) rounds during the few peak days of spring flooding.

Meanwhile, across town the Bow was having sport with bridges and residential areas such as Sunnyside. One memorable year it even lapped at the wooden steps of the Queen's Hotel on Eighth Avenue East. The Bow, at its worst, was a vicious part of the Calgary scene. At its best, it was a brawny servant that generated electricity and floated Eau Claire Lumber Company logs from Kananaskis country, a service it performed for fifty-eight years right up to 1944.

Temper tantrums have not harmed the Bow River's relationship with this community. Despite several dams on its short journey from the mountains, the river still moves through here at a vigorous, though perhaps less menacing, pace. And no longer do we burden it with intolerable wastes, for our cleansing system is one of North America's finest. But before we learned enough about the river, the extent of its angry outbursts gave us some considerable frights.

One of them threatened to physically involve Calgary in midsummer 1923. A storm, peaking around Bearspaw, took only minutes to gouge eleven kilometres of mainline CPR track, leaving washouts as deep as seven metres once the nine-metre overflow of floodwaters subsided. The Bow's rampage was so bad that east- and west-bound trains had to be rerouted through the Crowsnest Pass for most of four days. Of course the river left a trail of debris, mud, waterlogged roads and bridges (along with very worried next-of-kin) in its wake as it surged through Calgary.

One of the Bow River's more capricious adventures caused some abnormally red faces at city hall. Perhaps, if you travel east and west along that western extension to Memorial Drive from Twenty-fifth to Thirty-seventh streets west called Parkdale Boulevard, you may have seen an island in the Bow River that still wears, as it has for sixty years, a rather disreputable look. It began life as a midstream gravel island with a covering of bushes and some rather brave trees despite the constant battering it took from the swirling currents of the Bow. The small slice of land enjoyed many names, including Williams Island, Strawberry, Archer's, and Graves Island. Around 1913 English town planner Thomas H. Mawson, who wanted to recreate Calgary as the Venice of the North because of its rivers, proposed using the island as a stepping stone between Parkdale and Lowery's Garden and surrounding parkland at the foot of Spruce Cliff.

By 1932 the City of Calgary had a plan of its own for the island. For weeks machines dug the core out of the finger of land, shaping its gravel into a holding pond for water, naturally filtered by the gravel. They intended to pump the water that accumulated into a new steel water tower on Twentieth Avenue at Tenth Street NW. Communication between the Bow River and the city fathers was obviously tenuous, for the river won the discussion over this unseemly intrusion by demolishing the undertaking before the scheme had even been tested.

The Bow seems to have had "a thing" about islands. There used to be three islands in its path through Calgary–St. George's, St. Andrew's, and St. Patrick's. St. Andrew's disappeared years ago by joining itself to its upstream companion, St. Patrick's–for years a pleasant campground for Calgary visitors. The largest, more durable St. George's, was the site of Frank D. Wilson's farm for a time, although it, too, kept getting drenched in springtime. In 1891, having bought the three islands from the federal government for one dollar each, the city began clearing the compact tangle of wilderness that had taken over Wilson's abandoned farm. Today a more mannerly Bow, very damned and partly decimated by the diversion into the drinking systems of Calgary and Airdrie, struggles to regain its dominance over our bridges, and to retain its old enviable reputation as one of this continent's finest trout fishing streams.

Both of our cantankerous rivers have brought us as much pleasure as they have headaches. Some of my fondest memories are of the Elbow Valley in pre-Glenmore Lake days. It was a youngster's paradise. Narrow pathways snaked through the heavily treed valley all along the serpentine course of the stream. There was the very popular Rotary Hut, donated for camping and picnicking by the service club. There were backwaters for swimming, especially near Weaselhead's beaver dam. And the valley farm beneath the lake belonged to pioneer settler Sam Livingston, who named the place after Glen Malure in County Wicklow not far from his birthplace. Our rivers were, and continue to be, Calgary's garland of jewels.

Hooves on the Highways

IN THE DAYS BEFORE CALGARY EXISTED, THE only horses in these parts were Indian ponies with a market value of twenty to forty dollars. Apparently, until the mounties arrived, well-bred horses were scarce in southern Alberta.

Then, in the early 1880s, ranchers realized they could make money raising good quality mounts for the British Army, which had an insatiable appetite for war horses. When they heard this, the two Hull brothers, W.R. and J.R., who had been raising horses in the interior of British Columbia, headed east in 1883 herding 1200 horses to foothills country by way of the Crowsnest Pass.

They sold some to the mounted police in Calgary and the balance to the locally based Northwest Cattle Company. At this time one of our foothills spreads, the Quorn Ranch, imported a number of fine mares and sires, including some bearing names dedicated horsemen recognize to this day: Eagle Plume, Silk Gown, and Acrostic.

Thus, many fine cavalry horses were bred here, on land described by the chief federal veterinarian in these words: "Probably no better horse breeding country exists in the British Empire than the district of Alberta." But, for a while, the British Army demand shrivelled, and many Quorn-bred animals ended up as farm work horses.

The Cochrane and Stimson ranches at High River bred and raised purebreds and crossbreeds representative of the Irish Hunter, Clydesdale, Hackney, and Thoroughbred. The scrubby Indian Cayuse was displaced, and from about 1888, all the mounted police needs were met right here at home. This was due largely to Frank Strong of Fort Macleod and the Northwest Cattle Company, who bought most of the Hull brothers' herd.

The market was strong because land settlement, the Klondike gold rush, and the Boer War created new demands, raising prices into the $150 range. Gold prospectors were eager to pick up any animal that could carry a heavy pack, and hundreds of new immigrants created a demand for farm work-horses. There was also an expanding market for heavy draught-horses for mining and lumbering work.

In 1902 the Alberta Horsebreeders' Association made an interesting move. It persuaded the provincial government to limit the importation of cheap horses, closing the door to animals of mongrel lineage. The discrimination of Alberta ranchers and breeders began to pay off.

In 1901 the Pan-American Exhibition world's champion Hackney came from Alberta. In 1904, at the St. Louis World's Fair, both the champion Hackney stallion and mare came from our province. North America's largest and finest Percheron herd was owned by George Lane on the Bar U Ranch at Pekisko west of High River.

A "horsey" Englishman who wrote copiously of his visit to Alberta in 1912 was S.L. Bensusan. Later, while visiting a friend in a small Sussex town, he encountered a particularly fine draught-horse pulling one of the town carts. He noted:

> . . . clearly it was built for strength and endurance but, in addition to this, it had more beauty that one associates with the Suffolk Punch type of horse from which it was evidently descended. Moreover the satin-like quality of its skin proclaimed its fine condition.
>
> The man in charge was shovelling debris from the street and the horse responded equally to his voice and a wave of his hand. Naturally I, interested in good horseflesh, and in a small way, an owner and breeder, spoke to the man and congratulated him on the possession of such a handsome and mild-mannered animal of marked intelligence.
>
> "Yes, he is indeed a beauty," replied the man, "and strange to say he isn't English bred at all. He has come from the prairie out in Canada."

Apparently Mr. Bensusan was not surprised, for he had written: "In Calgary there is a ready market for drivers and saddle horses, while a turf club and hunt club contribute to the interest taken in horses . . . "

Interest indeed. In my young days, furniture moving vans were pulled by teams of giant horses. Daily delivery of bread and dairy foods was a job for horse-drawn wagons that cruised the entire city. Burns and Company had a fleet of spotless red-and-gold enamelled delivery wagons with impeccably groomed horse teams and whitecoated drivers. The shiny, matching horse-powered delivery fleet of the Hudson's Bay Company spanned the city.

Twice a day the railway's horse-drawn drays and wagons shuttled between the CPR baggage, express, and freight sheds strung along Ninth Avenue East and West at trackside and commercial establishments throughout the city. Deliveries and pickups included baggage transfer—handling rail passengers' luggage between residences and the depot free of charge.

The City of Calgary was a great user of horses for all of its earth-moving dump-wagons, its street-watering carts, street-cleaning, and garbage-collecting vehicles. The watering carts were very large, grey-painted wooden barrels. The teamster, on a high perch at the front, skilfully operated levers and pedals to avoid sprinkling pedestrians and the occasional motor car. He replenished his supply at fire hydrants. The broad flat spray, as he and his two horses trundled along the roads, stirred little dust eddies and left the kind of shallow mud that barefooted little boys loved to squinch in as they followed the cart like seagulls trailing a ponderous ocean liner.

One vivid memory from those days is of Springbank farmers hauling loads of hay, piled to great heights on ricks with spindly wheels that tottered along the gravelled Seventeenth Avenue West hill en route to the stockyards or midtown stables.

There was a grassy vacant lot at the foot of our street, empty but for a small windowless hut that housed a cast-iron hand-pump for a well. Indians from Sarcee stopped their democrats there to drop off their small children and a solemn-faced grandmother who was placed in charge. Then the young adults would clip-clop their way into town where they tethered their rigs behind billboards lining three sides of the block now occupied by Eaton's.

Mr. Bensusan made one more gem of a comment in his account of us and our town. "In a country where riding and driving are part of the normal exercise of a healthy man and woman,

Sergeant Ralph S. Kendall, RNWMP, astride his horse, Robin, 1910. Alberta ranchers sold many of their horses to the mounties. Kendall, in addition to being a fine judge of horseflesh, was author of a couple of wild west frontier adventure novels. *Courtesy Glenbow-Alberta Institute/NA-1265-1*

there is no need to fear that the coming of the aeroplane, which is nearly due, or the popularity of the motor car, already long established, will do aught to reduce a certain demand for horseflesh for pleasure. There are too many lovers of the horse, who regard the automobile as an accessory to business, and use it only when they are in a hurry."

Oh, Mr. Bensusan, if only you could try out Memorial Drive, Deerfoot Trail, or the Macleod Trail at rush hour today.

One Size Misfits All

I HAVE NEVER TRIED IT BUT I UNDERSTAND it is possible to conquer a fear of pompous, overbearing people by mentally picturing them naked, revealing all the lumps, bulges, and shortcomings that normal flesh is heir to. It would make a delightful and, in some carefully chosen instances, a somewhat titillating pastime; on the other hand, it could be a most disabling and destructive discovery. In any event, today's clothing can be either an excellent disguise, if chosen wisely, or a shattering revelation. Unfortunately, these days, the latter seems to be more common.

We were not perfect dressers back in my day, although the choice of youngsters' daily clothing usually projected parental good taste and firm guidance–qualities that seem woefully lacking today. Mind you, then (as now) clothing was used to cloak some horrible secrets.

One such garment was the binder. Perhaps it was a holdover from my mother's uncompromising upbringing, but I remember her dressing my sister and me in these contraptions, which we wore for many of our tenderest years without daring to rebel. A binder was a woolly, knitted belly-band, ten or twelve centimetres in width. It was seamless and bore a small red-and-white ticket denoting its maker. That tab grew pale with many rough trips up and down the ribbed glass scrubbing board that leaned, steaming and soapy, against the edge of the galvanized washtub in the gloom of the basement on laundry day.

After a bath the binder was stretched to slide over your head and snugly encircle your middle. I heard later that it was designed (a) to keep you warm in winter, and (b) to keep your bellybutton from jutting unnaturally as you matured. Fortunately, long before puberty stumbled your way, you outgrew your three or four binders, which by that time had outlived their elasticity.

As a young male you went on to simpler and more logical clothing. Your sister, however, was not so fortunate. For "dressed-up" occasions, she graduated to white cotton stockings, garters, and camisoles, and a higher kind of super-binder since training bras had not yet been invented.

On Saturdays and holidays around home you and your siblings lived in coveralls. They were of blue denim with a high, snug collar, no belt, long sleeves, stoutly sewn pockets, and embossed metal buttons all the way down the front, each saying "Union Made." Their design was completely sexless.

Coveralls, no underwear, and low-cut running shoes that smelled since the second day you wore them, and, perhaps, a broad-brimmed "cowfeed" straw hat was the attire of most kids on the block. There was no nourishment for sexual, social, or racial discrimination.

One of the more horrible garments of long-ago was the bathing suit. It was shapelessly constructed of navy blue cotton jersey with white

Sylvan Lake Bathers, ca. 1923. *Courtesy Glenbow-Alberta Institute/NC-6-411*

piping around its scoop neck, skirt, and short sleeves. When dry, it hid most flaws, for it had the gracefulness of a carelessly erected tent. When wet, the bathing suit appeared to be spray-painted on the bather's body. That was especially true at a well-remembered time in the 1920s when designers shocked a large segment of the public by eliminating the bathing-suit skirt.

Then, more than ever, it clung where nothing should cling in public places, nor, come to think of it, in private places. There seemed to be a one-size-misfits-all air about it, and those unfortunate people of substandard dimensions, their imperfections cruelly emphasized, were victims of the suit's soggy, saggy grasp.

At one stage, bold bathers purchased suits with

scarlet piping–a pretty daring move. Bathing caps were something else. The men's style was the grandparent of today's scuba-diver's helmet; women's caps were usually of brightly coloured rubber with contrasting petalled flowers or serrated frills, with a chin strap that snapped tight, for it was imperative that hair be kept dry.

Winter outer garments were definitely sexist. For men there was the Mackinaw coat of blanket cloth, thigh-length with a generous collar and elasticized cuffs. Women wore fur or fur-trimmed "bum-freezers," barely thigh-long, usually with high collars that seemed as deep as the coats. A cloche hat and high-heeled black or grey overboots trimmed with dyed rabbit fur completed the ensemble.

Adult males had a choice of all-felt boots, which because of their destructibility, had to be worn with galoshes when a chinook descended upon Calgary. Office workers wore low-cut Oxford shoes as long as the weather allowed, adding pearl-grey or taupe three-button spats or "ankle blankets" as we dubbed them. Heavy snowfalls forced them to don black jersey-and-rubber overshoes that fit snugly, as the name implied, over the shoes and fastened with one to four clasps depending upon the height of the boots.

A unisex wintertime necessity for those who rated comfort above style was the tip-to-toe suit of underwear known variously as long johns, combinations, or a union suit. Women as well as men favoured the encompassing garment with its front column of buttons, its knitted, ribbed arm and leg cuffs, and a convenient lid at the back that opened downwards and buttoned at each top corner.

In the depths of winter the white or ivory-tinted union suit was further enriched with a fleece lining. It was great for outdoor use, but on a shopping trip or a visit to a well-heated home it was efficient enough to bring on an attack of the vapours! Moreover, the sight of it must have created great emotional turmoil on the threshold of an intimate romantic encounter.

For years my schoolday summer garb had been long socks and short pants with bare knees. In winter I wore "long-handled" fleece-lined combinations over high stockings that vanished into the cuffs of riding breeches I loathed. I remember donning my first pair of formal long trousers to impress the girls at the age of thirteen. My mother and father, apparently seeking to prolong my childhood days, were most reluctant to agree to this "party wear."

By the time we, in turn, became the despair of high school teachers, fake coonskin coats and beanie caps in school colours were almost mandatory for the boys. The girls' fashion was the high-collared blouse, cardigan sweater, lavishly pleated skirt, and two-tone saddle shoes.

Oh, Rah! Rah! Rah!

Our Cathedral Was a Pro

AN OASIS OF HISTORY AND TRADITION stands quietly amid the bustling and ever-changing face of downtown Calgary. On the north-east corner of First Street East and Seventh Avenue stands the Cathedral Church of the Redeemer. Not outstanding for its impressive architecture, height, or size, this old heartbeat of the Anglican Church in Calgary is an enduring part of the city scene.

It and its predecessors have occupied that piece of land since the days when Fort Calgary's garrison policed all but the settlement adjoining it. It was within the Fort Calgary palisade that Rev. John W. Tims arrived to hold a Church of England service. Worshippers sat on planks supported on nail kegs to participate in the first of the denomination's services held in this part of the West.

In 1883 John Tims had been sent by his superiors in England to minister to the Indians at Blackfoot Crossing in the northwest wilderness of Canada. After a remarkably swift six-week journey from Oxford the young man of twenty-six arrived, ready to begin his missionary work.

Shortly after his arrival among the Blackfoot, Rev. Tims received a request to come further west to conduct a service for Anglicans in the settlement of Calgary. In order to get there on time, Tims had to travel from the whistle-stop of Gleichen, with the engineer and fireman, on the footplate of a westbound freight locomotive.

The summons was by no means an indication that his base of operations would be shifted to Calgary. However, it did mark the beginning of the role of the Church of England (its earlier name) in the religious life of our foothills community.

Anglicans here were most anxious to complete construction of their church ahead of a group in Pincher Creek who also sought the honour of building the first church in the planned Anglican Diocese of Calgary. Actually, the Pincher Creek congregation did complete its project a week ahead of the Calgarians, but the bishop was an economical cleric. He was already in Calgary so first he dedicated the Church of the Redeemer, then made the coach trip to Pincher Creek.

The Calgary church was dedicated in August 1884, and its well-being left in the care of Rev. E. Paske Smith. He was backed by a group whose title was so typical of the era's apprehension of the "primitive" world: the Society for the Propagation of the Gospel in Foreign Parts. The first service he conducted was at Easter, 1884, in the modest white clapboard cruciform structure with its small rose window above the front porch and its steep-roofed bell-tower. It held about sixty worshippers.

For a time, the intersection of Osler Street and McIntyre Avenue (First Street and Seventh Avenue East) was distinctly ecclesiastical. On one corner was the Anglican church, and to the west, across Osler before the Beveridge Block took over the space, was the Methodist church and parsonage.

Church of England (Anglican) Pro-Cathedral of the Redeemer on Seventh Avenue at First Street East. The cornerstone was laid in 1904. *Courtesy Glenbow-Alberta Institute/NA-2643-6*

The southeast corner housed the Salvation Army Citadel. It is said that on hot summer Sunday mornings, with all windows and doors open, three congregations battled for the honour of being the lustiest, although not necessarily the most melodic, evangelical group to shatter the settlement's calm.

An expanding congregation warranted an enlargement of the Church of the Redeemer in 1887, and the extent of the church's influence was even more enhanced by the arrival, in 1900, of Rev. E.C. Paget, who served as rector until being appointed dean. In tribute to his great work in the parish, red brick Paget Hall was built to the east of the church and swiftly became the hub of secular parish activities.

In its earliest years it housed a church school, and women of the parish met there under Mrs. Willoughby Cummings and Miss Louey Paterson, who was brought out from Toronto in 1890 as a staff church worker. Not being set aside as a cathedral in those early days, the church became known as the Pro-Cathedral, a title that stuck for nearly half a century.

When Bishop H.R. Ragg arrived on the scene he realized it was impossible for Calgary's Anglican community to raise the amount necessary for a full-scale cathedral of traditional British Isles style. In an admirable compromise, he made possible full cathedral status for "The Pro" in 1949.

In the meantime, the wooden church had been replaced by today's sandstone cathedral announced as a one-thousand-seat place of worship, erected at a cost of about eighty-three thousand dollars. It was consecrated in the autumn of 1905. My own family entered that church's picture when my mother came from England to join her fiancé. Soon after, on 5 September 1909, she and my father were married at the Pro-Cathedral.

One of the interesting features of the present church is its acoustic quality. Years before Calgary had acoustically designed and engineered concert halls and auditoriums of modest proportions, the Canadian Broadcasting Corporation aired many classical solo and ensemble programs from "The Pro" enhanced by the rich resonance resulting from its heavy walls and aged beams and panelling.

The Gothic influence of its design—narrow, arched stained-glass windows, vaulted beaming, regimental colours, and memorial wall tablets—combine to make the simple, dignified church a midtown spiritual haven. Especially heartwarming have been its years of noontime recitals for the brown-bag office workers and the dreary-hearted, in search of its consoling and unchanging ambience in a tumultuous world.

While the sandstone "mother" church trembles at the constant tramping of passing LRT trains and a swarm of buses off to the south, St. Paul's Church, on the northern rim of Midnapore, shudders at the torrent of vehicles at its doorstep along #2 Highway.

Little St. Paul's, consecrated in 1885, a miniature replica of the original Church of the Redeemer, has seen a bewildering reshaping of its surroundings. Erected as a country village church in the old settlement of Midnapore, the first stop south of Calgary, St. Paul's was built from the same set of blueprints as its wooden "parent" on Seventh Avenue.

Parishioners in those days were area ranchers and farmers. Their contributions made it possible for their little rural church to acquire stained-glass windows, traditional oak furnishings, and a bell that had been calling the faithful to prayer at a southern English village church for two hundred years. And in the little churchyard beside St. Paul's in Midnapore, diminutive offspring of the Church of the Redeemer, are gravestones marking the final resting place of Archdeacon John and Mrs. Tims.

You Didn't Mess with Mother Fulham

CAROLINE FULHAM WAS PROBABLY THE most notorious of Calgary's pioneer settlers. Her husband, John, never achieved the measure of distinction enjoyed by his boisterous wife and must have found it uncomfortable to live in her ample shadow.

The Fulhams lived in a small white bungalow on McIntyre Avenue just west of Ross Street (Seventh and Fourth Street West) at the back of today's Court House. Caroline, obviously wearing the family pants, kept an assortment of livestock behind the picket fence that partly surrounded the property.

Her most useful animal was a horse that pulled wooden barrels aboard a wagon. Mother Fulham made daily raucous rounds of the town's restaurants and hotels collecting discarded food she used as swill for her pigs. It is said she easily hoisted loaded barrels onto her wagon and shouted coarse warnings to anyone unfortunate enough to get in her way. The horse, some pigs, and a cow constituted her backyard livestock collection.

The cow was the most troublesome of all. It developed a habit of wandering off the property, appearing to prefer the wild fodder that grew along the CPR tracks a few blocks south of the Fulham house. One day the inevitable occurred. The cow wandered onto the tracks and was demolished by a passing train.

Caroline Fulham hired Calgary's fiery young Irish lawyer Paddy Nolan to handle her lawsuit for damages. Her anger at the railway's negligence became part of the Fulham legend. The CPR lawyers maintained there was an obvious "NO TRESPASSING" sign at the scene of the cow's demise. In court Mrs. Fulham thundered, "Ya damn fools, you think me cow could read?"

She was invited to a "peace conference" aboard the private car of CPR president Van Horne during one of his stopovers. Tearfully she refused his offer of a replacement cow, and, although they are said to have parted on reasonably friendly terms, she bad-mouthed the company for the rest of her days in Calgary.

One day, in her own unique way, the unsinkable woman won a bet with pioneer Dr. Harry Goodsir Mackid. He was examining her injured leg, which he found to be exceptionally filthy. He exploded, "I'll bet you five dollars, Mrs. Fulham, there isn't a dirtier leg in all of Calgary."

"You're on!" she retorted, and pulled up her skirt to reveal her equally filthy other leg. Dr. Mackid paid the bet.

Caroline Fulham added to her colourful reputation in those days long before the liberation of women by proving her well-earned status in the community. She was the only woman in Calgary who would, and did, belly up to the all-male stronghold of the Alberta Hotel bar, and always matched the men drink-for-drink.

The bar at the Alberta Hotel, ca. 1900. Caroline Fulham was among the many Calgarians who came here to quench their thirst. *Courtesy Glenbow-Alberta Institute/NA-654-4*

Early in the century advancing age caught up with Caroline Fulham. She left Calgary to spend the remainder of her days at the Pacific coast, but she had left her indelible mark on Calgary and all those who knew her.

Trains You Loved to Hate

HERE IS THE SCENARIO: IT IS A HOT AFTERnoon in 1935. You are working at your office desk on the second floor at the rear of 221 Eighth Avenue West. You plan to meet someone special after work, so have placed your broad-brimmed white hat and white gloves carefully atop the filing cabinet. Your newly dry-cleaned white linen coat hangs on a nearby coat rack.

It is quiet except for the swish of papers, the harsh clacking of your Royal typewriter, and the buzzing of a bluebottle fly that hasn't the sense to swoop down instead of up. The lower part of the big unscreened window is open, propped high on a wooden stick.

Suddenly there is a clanking and clashing down below in the back lane. You can hardly hear yourself think for the huffing and puffing. You hurtle to the window to shut it, but, alas, you are too late. Your lovely white things, your desk, your papers, all have that peppered look as tiny cinders and flecks of soot settle over everything. Down there, along the lane between Eighth and Ninth avenues, a thumping steam railway engine is yanking at a short string of boxcars. It stops and, right below your window, pants heavily to regain its breath. Then, with a series of cinder-laden belches, it moves east or west along the lane, spotting boxcars at the loading docks of neighbourhood warehouses.

In the early years only a few businesses clustered along the new train tracks, but eventually it reached a point where vehicular and pedestrian traffic was held up several times a day as trains passed by. Then, in time, strings of freight cars chuffed along the Eighth/Ninth Avenue lane and across the streets between about First Street East and Seventh Street West on the north side of the railway's main line, and between Tenth and Eleventh avenues on the south side.

The biggest headaches of all were caused by the delays across Fourth Street West. Not only were boxcars shunted between units of the Robin Hood Flour Mill, whose plant straddled Fourth, but they also blocked the street north of there as loads were eased along the back lane. Of course, in those days Fourth Street was not a subway but a multitrack level crossing. It was a dominant factor in the well-being of Calgary's midtown life, and a constant bristly topic of conversation.

In addition to the mainline tracks with their heavy schedule of cross-country passenger runs and freight trains, there was a gaggle of busy sidings. From high in a skinny wooden tower on the east side of the crossing a man controlled candystriped wooden arms equipped with red lanterns, lowering or raising them to the accompaniment of a loud clanging bell. They protected the main line and a few passing tracks. Often the arms–long ones for vehicular traffic, short ones blocking off the wooden sidewalks–would just reach the upright

Downtown Calgary in 1929. Warehouses, serviced by back-lane railway tracks, line Ninth, Tenth, and Eleventh avenues through the centre of the city's business core. *Lorne Burkell photo*

all-clear position when along would come a little shunting engine with another string of cars, noisily claiming the right-of-way.

Close to the outside edges of the level crossing, on the north, was a pair of unguarded sidings within the Robin Hood property where boxcars loaded with grain or flour were shuffled back and forth, invariably at "rush hour." On the southern side, just when you felt you had finally cleared the hurdle, you would encounter the shunting along the back lane between Tenth and Eleventh avenues.

Considering Calgary's size back then, north-south road traffic was reasonably heavy. This was because the only subways (grade separations in today's jargon) were at Second and First streets East, and at First and Eighth streets West. Every other crossing represented an uneven meeting of willpower between rail trains, road vehicles, and pedestrians, who were constantly imperiling themselves by ducking under the barriers and nipping across the tracks in the shadow of oncoming trains and vehicles.

Horse-drawn and motor freight-haulers were in the infancy stage so rail transportation was of paramount importance. The constant interruption by trains caused a lot of fretting and a succession of threats to invoke a law limiting the time a train could dally at a crossing. The sooty and cindery back lane traffic was "one of those things." The smoke, dirt, and noise were a price that had to be paid for the movement of merchandise.

Back then, where the mall today leads a comparatively peaceful retail and banking life, the south side of Eighth Avenue East and West, backing onto the land shared with Ninth Avenue, contained almost as many warehouses as retail and office establishments. Unlovely, grubby little freight locomotives would spot loads of china and glass for Prudden's down near Centre Street, carpets for Jordan's just west of First Street, for Pain's Furs next to the Alberta Hotel, and the Brock dry goods wholesale warehouse at Second Street. Back-door to back-door with Brocks was one of the city's largest Ford dealerships, which received all its new vehicles by back-lane rail.

In the late 1920s, at Eighth Street and Eleventh Avenue, Ford established a regional warehouse as well. It backed onto the south-side rail supply line that served such businesses as the Winnipeg firm of Stephens Paints, the Pedlar People, General Electric at its very big warehouse at Fourth Street and Eleventh Avenue, Sylvester Supply, and a westward-reaching string of construction suppliers such as the Crown and Cushing lumber companies on the same avenue to about Fourteenth Street West.

Back over at Ninth Avenue, served by the more northerly back-lane line, was Plunkett and Savage, which shipped carloads of vegetables and fruit in and out of the city. Another big railway customer and near neighbour of the Grain Exchange Building was the Ninth Avenue factory of Great West Saddlery. Every other day it took delivery of boxcar loads of hides, rope, and twine, and shipped bulk orders of harnesses, horse collars, and saddles to country dealers.

Further west along Eighth and Ninth avenues, wholesalers of plumbing and heating supplies, stoves and furnaces, and road-building machinery loaded and unloaded their heavy goods along the narrow corridor. Earlier in the century a farm machinery dealer opposite today's TD Square, had tractors and automobiles shipped in by rail to his open air "showroom" lot adjoining his warehouse, encouraging agricultural customers to drive their purchases off the lot, through town, and out to their farms.

Office workers in the area acquired a certain immunity to the noise, but in those summer days before air conditioning the only relief from the stifling heat was an open window. That was the pre-diesel era, too. The "second-floor-back" office people in the Leeson-Lineham Block, and the Alberta, McDougall, Ward, and Maclean blocks put up with a lot. They were about level with the upturned maw of a shunting locomotive's stack.

Those stubby little steam engines had a diabolical capability of burping a geyser of cindery dust just as you were taking in a much-needed "breath of fresh air." It seemed to happen on cue. I know, from having been caught several times. It was great for the dry-cleaning fraternity, but it almost shattered my lifelong love affair with trains.

Making Music

CALGARY'S EARLY MUSIC MAKERS WERE A unique and assorted bunch. Many made a lasting name for themselves in the days when the city was small and a lot of its musical gatherings were social milestones.

One such musician was Jean McWilliam, a boarding-house keeper in early Calgary said to have been the first police matron. She was offered a two-year contract, along with her musical siblings, Johnny and Molly, to play on the Pantages vaudeville circuit. James "Cappy" Smart, for many years our fire chief, was a ham actor and amateur musician who regaled his fellow townsmen with his talents at the drop of a hat.

Speaking of amateur musicians, long-time Calgarian Harry Chritchley reminded me of Jim Davidson. He bought the Regent pipe-organ when the Hudson's Bay Company decided about 1928 to enlarge its Seventh Avenue department store south to Eighth Avenue, meaning the demise of Temple-Duff Drugs and the Regent, formerly Pantages, Theatre. Jim had the organ moved into his new house on Royal Avenue where he played to his heart's content, but, because of the instrument's bulk, he could not play in public.

Russell Gideon, a large black man apprenticed with McDermid Drugs, arrived in Calgary in the 1930s, a veteran of World War I, and a graduate of Duke University where he had played football to finance his pharmacy career. He played ball with the Calgary Tigers, and loved taking all summer off to play drums with Hobart Cowan's orchestra at Penley's Varsity Hall dance pavilion at Sylvan Lake.

A *Calgary Herald* Linotype operator, Stanley Cummer, another World War I veteran, was also a drummer. He played with Ma Trainor's dance band at the Avenue Ballroom across the street from Eaton's midtown department store. Cyril Godwin conducted the pit orchestra at the new Capitol Theatre where TD Square stands today. Godwin was replaced, around 1938, by Cecil Kappey and His Kapitolians.

Kappey carved quite a niche for himself as a conductor, pianist, and organist. He created his own job as "staff pianist" at the *Calgary Herald*'s radio station, CFAC. As such, he was organist at Christ Church, Elbow Park, for the weekly half-hour radio program *The Vesper Hour* on which Rev. George Luxton read inspirational poetry and Cecil played suitable background music. Luxton went on, without the glamour of local velvet-voiced radio stardom, to become Anglican Bishop of Rupert's Land.

When Cyril Godwin was setting up the new Capitol Theatre, he held orchestra auditions. The tenor singer chosen to put words to the thirty-five-piece orchestral music was London-born Harold DeCaux, a Huguenot descendant who had lived in Calgary most of his life. Handily, Harold also was quite a good horn player, so he could double in the

Dances were a major social event in early Calgary. The folks in this photo have stepped out to enjoy themselves at the Pharmaceutical Association Ball held in the Palliser Hotel. *Courtesy Glenbow-Alberta Institute/NA-4019-8*

band. That sort of flexibility, in those days, could determine whether you got a booking or were relegated to canned soup on a hotplate.

Harold sang gigs with Ted Williams's orchestra, which played for dances at the Canadian Legion hall on Seventh Avenue, and that's where the new management of the about-to-be-opened Capitol heard him. Billed by the theatre as "The Nightingale Tenor of the Air," Harold became better known as "The Singing Waiter," because between waiting tables at the Palliser Hotel, he was perhaps the busiest local pop tenor singer of the 1920s. Harold became the hotel's maitre d', but the promotions never stopped him from singing.

Another musician who never seemed to stop was Bankhead-born Louis Trono, another hotelier, who worked his way from Banff Springs busboy at the age of seventeen to leader of its house band. Louis was a contemporary of musicians like bassist Elmer Peck, clarinetist Ted Harvey, violist Earl Ruttan, banjoist Ted Fisher and trumpeters Wick Ford and Fred Athey. And there were many more, for Calgary was home to numerous popular music makers.

Rarely did the musicians make much of a living with their music. They were paid frugally and usually existed on little more than tips. They played in places such as the Plaza in the basement of the Lougheed Building, the Mandarin Gardens near the station on Centre Street, on amateur talent nights at the Variety and Capitol theatres, and especially on festive dates at the Palliser, as well as the dance pavilions at Bowness and Chestermere Lake in the summer.

There were never enough jobs to go round, especially since only theatre pit orchestras, Penley's Dancing Academy, the Chestermere and Bowness pavilions, and, in season, the dance floors at Sylvan and Gull Lakes, Waterton, and Banff provided much more than one-night stands. Broadcasting provided extra work for some otherwise starving musicians such as Peck, Curley Nixon, John Bullough, Harry Hutchcroft, Josh Henthorn, Bus Totten, Si Hopkins, Ted Forsey, Lou Darby, and Jac Friedenburg. Who got the gig depended upon which music style was in demand at the time: cowboy hoe-down, ballroom dance, background band, or whatever else. The fee that organizers of these musical events set aside for the orchestra was skimpy to say the least.

One example of an eagerly accepted "extra" was the very flamboyant opening of the Spiller Flour Mill at Bonnybrook on the way to Ogden. The British company that built the huge new plant was anxious to make its mark and it did just that. On the night of 7 September 1927, Spiller the Millers staged a bash. On each of three of the mill's polished oak floors (before all the flour milling machinery had been installed) there was dancing, acres of it, plus a buffet on each level. Bus Totten, Louis Trono, and Wick Ford were hired to assemble an orchestra assigned to one of the three floors. Everyone in Calgary received an invitation, 66,000 potential guests. It was a whopping success.

Mart Kenny and His Western Five, later his Western Gentlemen, secured a summer-long contract in Calgary prompting them to move here from Vancouver. They lived in Elbow Park for a while. The band rented a house near today's Glencoe Club while playing seasonal gigs. Following a Mart Kenny run, Moxie Whitney played for many seasons at the Banff Springs Hotel between 1947 and 1963, but each big band leader had his established players and the mountain hotels were only open four months of the year. So those activities were of little benefit to Calgary instrumentalists.

However, the local musicians persevered; very few left for allegedly greener pastures. Thanks to their persistence, and their love for their work, their music put lilts into the hearts of yesterday's Calgarians.

The Basics Were Best

IT IS ALWAYS CONSOLING TO MEET SOMEONE with whom you went to school. Such an encounter reassures me that in fact I did go to school, although nothing much came of it. I recall my father mocking my inattentiveness by suggesting that the only way I would ever graduate from grade five would be by marrying the teacher.

Fort Calgary had been in existence for nine years before there were sufficient children in the nearby settlement to warrant the establishment of a school. The first classes were held by John W. Costello in 1883 in Boynton Hall on Stephen Avenue, but budgetary problems, even back then, ended the effort after only two months. The year 1885 marked the start of an official community effort to form a public school district that would be eligible for government financial help. A small cottage on (today's) Ninth Avenue and Fifth Street East became our first public school with Spencer Douglas as the teacher. Two more teachers and a janitor soon joined the staff.

A year later the first inspector arrived to examine the class, and submitted a most favourable report. John Maclean wrote in 1886:

> There were sixty pupils present, all of whom evinced deep interests in their studies. Their progress has been in general rapid. The order maintained in school is excellent. This has been secured by means of kindness and tact on the part of the teachers. A healthy tone pervades the department of study, the pupils trying to excel.

As Calgary grew so did its schools in number and size. I still remember my first day at Glengarry Cottage School (whose slightly modernized twin is still in existence on Fifth Avenue at about Twenty-third Street NW). Mislabelled a cottage, it had two rooms, one on the main floor, the other upstairs. The plumbing was in the otherwise naked basement where the furnace and the coal bin lurked along with the janitor's sink, mop, and pail. The classrooms were linked by an indoor and outdoor staircase, and a verandah stretched across the width of the building on the main floor. The place had enough of a military air about it to qualify as "standard school board issue."

The classrooms were identical, each big room with a high ceiling, blackboards covering two walls, and windows on the west wall. Behind the front blackboard was a narrow corridor with a low row of coat hooks along its entire length, at junior pupil height, of course. It was into that corridor, muffled by child-sized overcoats and galoshes, that one was banished for a specified number of minutes for bad behaviour. The fourth classroom wall, in addition to the entrance door, sported bulletin boards displaying works of art, assorted show-and-tell items on long-term display, and notices in large print, which we were supposed to learn to read and relay home.

It was education at its simplest. Depending upon the split in enrolment, the grade one pupils occupied the individual desks on one side of the room, the grade two students were in the middle, and on the other side were those in grade three. It must have been a tiring job for the teacher—addressing part of the room at a time, making sure other segments were busy on projects while the rest were being instructed at their levels. But it worked, and it was about then that my individuality asserted itself.

For years my sister and I had been exposed to a nightly bedtime story, usually something by a well-known adventure writer such as Lewis Carroll, Rudyard Kipling, Rider Haggard, G.A. Henty. I began finding the grade one curriculum rather dull. One day I was a bit sulky over some simple assignment and so struck up a quiet conversation with the kid at the next desk. I was cut off in midsentence by Miss MacWilliams, who banished me to an empty desk across the room where, with the grade three kids, she could keep an eye on me. In mock isolation I was given the grade three item they were tackling, and never did go back, partly because the term was nearly over anyway. The following year the grade three reading, sentence-making, and story-telling assignments were fun, although, because I still think two and two make five, perhaps I should have been put back in my place.

It was a different world calling for a different curriculum. In simpler times the school courses were basically within the realm of the teacher's comprehension, and that person was charged with teaching one and all—the so-called dumb ones who plodded through every day, and the bright ones to whom school was a boring waste of time.

As for the premises, a school was either a cottage or its new close relative, a bungalow, and fit well into any neighbourhood. It was single storey, hip-roofed, made of local very rough dark brown cinder brick and had four classrooms and a principal's office. The latter also served as a place to chastise and mete out punishment to disobedient or bewildered kids, and a room for the teachers to gather to complain about "the system" and the curriculum, and to brown-bag it at noon. Local building materials and "sensible style" seemed to be the criteria. Of course there were no worries about parking, counselling, physical education, library, individual student lockers, or any other such "frills."

By 1910 Calgary had twenty-three schools. The larger ones resembled barracks built of local sandstone representing a one-million-dollar investment. Four new ones were on the drawing boards for construction in 1911, and, as a modern extra, they were to contain space for manual training for boys, and household science for girls.

Families who could afford it, financially and socially, chose the alternative routes of Western Canada School, an all-boys boarding and day school set-up that bore strong overtones of the English Public School system, with emphasis on physical as well as mental instruction. There was St. Hilda's School for Girls, another English-type boarding and day school institution where, as with the Western boys, a strict uniform code erased most of the discrepancies in family backgrounds.

There was the Church of England's Bishop Pinkham College in Hillhurst and, near the Armoury, the Methodist's strictly run Mount Royal College. Under the thumb of the moralist preacher Rev. George Kerby, courses were offered in commerce and shorthand, physical culture, and—

Grade six class at King Edward School, 1916. The teacher, seen here at the back of the class, is Miss Clint. *Courtesy Glenbow-Alberta Institute/NA-2517-3*

through its noted Conservatory of Music—the lively arts. We, in the run-of-the-mill public and high schools, were instructed in the basic "three Rs," plus in high school, some special emphasis on history, physics, chemistry, French, Latin, advanced mathematics, geography, geometry, literature, and composition.

In essence, schooling in those days was a Spartan, disciplined, quite inflexible, noncoddling experience. Within it you worked and thought and learned in order to survive. There was little room for doubt as to whose fault it was if you sank. I guess it wouldn't work today, but I'm convinced it sure did back then.

Our Daily Bread

BACK IN 2050 B.C. AN EGYPTIAN SLAVE MADE the delightful error of allowing some edibles to ferment, thereby discovering leavened bread. Today bread is one of our most popular foods, and, because it is consumed by nearly everyone, it has been abused by every food faddist in and out of Christendom.

A perennial complaint is the alleged lack of nutrition in white bread. However, it happens that on 2 February 1953, vitamin-enriched white bread appeared on the market throughout Canada. Flour millers, many of them based in Calgary, began enriching flour with extra vitamins: riboflavin, niacin, thiamin, and iron.

Some old-timers in Calgary will remember Shelley's Bakery with its house-to-house delivery. The company's mainstay was Butternut Bread—"Rich as butter, sweet as a Nut." "Milkmaid" bread was the Mitchell Bakery trademark when that firm had twelve household and commercial service delivery wagons.

One of Calgary's noteworthy breads, although not readily available to the general public, was the crusty roll that brought Palliser hotel dining much renown. Its steam-fed brick oven, originally constructed in 1914, was unique to Alberta. Its successor continues to supply the hotel with bakery foods, but since September 1991 the oven no longer turns out its crusty roll treats for hotel diners and off-premise customers.

Calgary's first two bakery firms appear to have been those of Kinniston and Company and the Warden Brothers, both of whose premises were on Stephen Avenue as long ago as 1901. A few doors away from their businesses was the bakeshop of Stirrett and Hoad. The City Bakery, on the northeast corner of Eighth Avenue and Second Street East, operated by Messrs. Arnell and Mills, supplied a walk-in-trade in 1906. Midblock, further to the east, was the Palmetto Bakery, which flourished for many years. To the east in the next block of Eighth Avenue was baker E. Jutras.

C.T. Gilbert, who had conducted his grocery and confectionery business on the northwest corner of Centre Street and Seventh Avenue, switched jobs and addresses to become half of a new City Bakery team. It occupied a spot on Eighth Avenue West where, in later years, there stood the stationery store owned and operated by one-time mayor Fred E. Osborne. The City Bakery still exists, performing a nostalgic seasonal baking business at Heritage Park.

As the city grew, larger and more successful bakeries acquired horses and wagons as a means of expanding their business into the suburbs, serving customers with daily kitchen-door delivery of bread and other bakery foods. Among them was John T. Mitchell whose bakery, in addition to the "Milkmaid" trademark, became popular because of its "Perfection" brand bread. The plant was close by the Elbow River at Fourteenth Avenue East beyond the sandstone building that had been Calgary's General, and later its Isolation, hospital. During World War I that building served as an army depot, then, in peacetime, became a bakery once again. Eventually, Weston's bakery products emerged from this location.

Scottish-born brothers, William and George Jackson, produced five thousand loaves of "Maltine" and "Bermaline" bread at their bakery on Eighth Street at Fifteenth Avenue West. The Golden West Bakery was another contender in the increasingly competitive market. On Hillhurst's Second Avenue NW was the Palace Bakery, which later expanded to a plant it built near the Mewata Armoury following a Hillhurst fire in 1940. Another famous and enduring bakery name with plants scattered throughout the west, has been that of the Vancouver-based McGavin organization. It has outlasted Canadian Bakeries, which, for years was called Shelley's 4X Bakery in Calgary.

For decades that old brick Shelley building occupying the northeast corner of Eleventh Street and Twelfth Avenue SW, was the home of a range of 4X products including, in addition to "Butternut" bread, its renowned Eccles cakes and currant buns. Daily, its horse-drawn rigs blanketed the ever-expanding retail core as well as the furthest corners of the sprawling suburbs.

Of course, all this time, independent little one-man or family bakery shops were opening in every community. The Victoria Bakery on Second Street East near Tenth Avenue must have been one of the grandparents of that coterie, for it existed in the identical location to serve the Victoria Park area customers for at least three-quarters of a century. Another of the old-timers on the bakery scene was Picardy's. It was started in Winnipeg by World War I veterans and enjoyed a booming business in many western cities. Two of its mauve-and-yellow stores thrived only a block apart on Eighth Avenue West in the 1930s. They were memorable for their fancy cakes, pies, pecan rolls, and other rich bakery snacks that lured many a downtown office worker during the coffee break.

Another bakery firm arising from the echoes of World War I was the National System of Baking. The Heagle brothers, Everard, Ernest, Harry, Fred, Walter, and Frank decided to tackle the bakery industry mainly because Walter had been a successful cook aboard a U.S. submarine. Walter, the leader of the sibling sextet, felt they had a system that would help them achieve national stature far beyond the confines of Calgary. Hence the name, National.

Their first bakery was on the east side of Centre Street bordering the lane in back of Eighth Avenue. In the large window was a revolutionary revolving bake oven recently invented and built in Toronto. Fired by natural gas, it slowly turned in Ferris-wheel fashion, and passersby could see, through rows of mica windows, trays of browning loaves. Cunningly, the Heagles installed an exhaust fan in the transom above the door. Thus customers not only could see the loaves cooking, they could savour the exotic aroma of fresh bread.

In almost no time the brothers opened two more identical shops in Calgary, as well as bakeries in Edmonton, Regina, Saskatoon, Lethbridge, Medicine Hat, Drumheller, Vancouver, Port Arthur, Ottawa, Kingston, St. Catharines, and Hamilton, where Walter moved and set up company headquarters. In time they had sixteen storefront bakeries, the last of which recently closed its doors in Calgary after the firm's seventy-one year lifetime.

Two things my old friend Frank Heagle assured

The Gilbert and Jay Bakery Shop on Stephen Avenue, 1900. *Courtesy Glenbow-Alberta Institute/NA-1458-2*

me years ago: even during the worst food shortages of World War II the firm never compromised quality. If real butter and whole milk and cream were not immediately available, the National System's ovens were allowed to cool until the situation was restored. The other thing that kept the company viable in the face of hefty competition was that if a store did not meet a profit mark of 1,500 loaves daily plus pastries, it was closed without regret.

One thing I know from my very active years with the baking industry trade association, the small "mom and pop shops" and the National never relied on "honkers" to maintain a good business. One of the tricks of the trade was convincing Mrs. Customer that the bread was fresh. Larger bakeries often threw diglycerides into the mix, which, while dietetically harmless, kept the baked loaf soft for days. The customer would squeeze the loaf–in other words–"Honk it!" to convince herself it was fresh because it was spongy.

Today all white flour is vitamin-enriched. So whether it honks or not, today's loaf of bread indeed is the "staff of life," a valuable and essential part of a well-laid meal table.

Stopping for the Red Lights

THOU RASCAL BEADLE, HOLD THY BLOODY hand! Why dost thou lash that whore?" asked Shakespeare's King Lear; but then, the beadles (parish officers) have been "lashing" members of the world's oldest profession since the dawn of mankind.

Our dearly beloved Calgary has never been an exception to the unrelenting pursuit of purity. Try though we may, we and our beadles never have attained that lily white state of grace. Some of our Calgary predecessors took a stab at it; some did not even try. For example, in 1888, Stephen Avenue furniture dealer A.E. Shelton, upon being "promoted" from alderman to mayor of the Town of Calgary and chairman of the Police and Relief Committee, gave his police chief strict instructions to leave gamblers and prostitutes alone. Not a single raid was recorded in 1888.

On the other hand, in 1910 Police Chief Thomas Mackie led the community's first large raid, a particularly successful one, on a two-storey Eighth Avenue "cafeteria" run by a notorious pair, Burt and Johnnie Reid. Many illegal drinkers and gamblers and a number of women "roomers" and "chambermaids" were arrested. Burt soon abandoned that line of work. However, his brother Johnnie moved the business to South Coulee (near today's Chinook Shopping Centre), thus transforming a respectable, quiet family suburb into a wide-open red light district.

The women who plied their trade in such establishments bore many names, nearly all of them false, of course. Some of the more notorious earned such handles as Lady Lily, Chesty O'Toole, Horizontal Hanna, and, when automobiles came into vogue, Parallel Parker.

One notorious madam wore her real name proudly. She was Pearl Miller, owner and operator of several houses of ill repute, as they were widely known in my young days. We youngsters kept an eye open for their trademark: a curved driveway with the inside of the arc between two gateways masked by bushes. That, the "big kids" told us, was for fast and easy access, discreet parking, and swift escape by car in the event of a raid.

At one time Pearl Miller had a "house" on Seventeenth Avenue near Twenty-sixth Street West, later on 6A Street in Elbow Park. Another, close to today's Heritage Drive and the Macleod Trail, was popular in the 1920s and 1930s with oil field workers moving to and from Turner Valley during its heyday of petroleum exploration. It was at that place that Bill Donlevy and his fellow railway telegraphers stopped for an innocent drink, in spite of the presence of an assortment of blondes, brunettes, and redheads whose interests and motives were somewhat more remunerative than a fifty-cent watered down drink. Bill reminisced, "Forced to vacate her Manchester mansion, Pearl moved her 'stable' to a more prestigious location—

Mount Royal. While the GI's had pep rallies: 'Remember Pearl Harbour,' the Calgary Tanks and Highlanders had their own 'To hell with Pearl Harbour, remember Pearl Miller.'"

Years earlier, Pearl Miller's business base was on Ninth Avenue East where a small row of look-alike cottages faced the then-extensive downtown CPR rail yard. Pearl had friends everywhere and in all walks of life, among them members of the railway's running trades. When Calgary author James H. Gray was researching his 1971 book *Red Lights on the Prairies*, he shared with me a merry tale he had come across.

Pearl Miller had been tipped off by an alert customer that the city police, armed with binoculars, were setting up a "command post" in a lone free-standing boxcar on a siding facing her main house. The officers, confided her informant, were about to log all the comings and goings of the girls' customers.

Pearl wasted no time phoning one of her train-crew friends. Before long a fussy little yard locomotive huffed up to the boxcar. A trainman clambered down from the steam engine's footplate, hustled over to the boxcar, rolled shut the partially opened door, fastened it, and signalled the engineer to inch

The Nose Creek brothels, located north of the railway bridge over the Bow River, conducted a thriving business from 1911 to 1913. *Courtesy Glenbow-Alberta Institute/NA-673-9*

Pearl Newton plied her trade in Calgary's early brothels, ca. 1915. *Courtesy Glenbow-Alberta Institute/NA-625-13*

back and couple onto the car. With it securely in tow, the "hijackers" steamed away in the direction of the Alyth freight yards where they left the boxcar. A while later Pearl was assured that the shouting, hot, and thoroughly frustrated spy team was released from the impromptu cell as the result of an anonymous tip-off.

Sometimes I have been asked by curious enemies if I have ever been inside such an establishment. My honest reply has to be "Yes, once, but it wasn't one of Pearl Miller's." We were in our mid-teens and the ringleader of our quartet was a doctor's son much older than his years and ours. It was during the Depression, and at that time some red light houses were in a tawdry row on Sixth Avenue East. One hot summer afternoon our "leader" was determined to visit a brothel for his own pleasure. He also insisted the experience was an important step in our maturation. Before I had time to collect my inhibitions I was tagging along.

He parked the car at the end of the block and, with three of us wide-eyed little lambs in tow, strode with panache towards his goal. At each wire gate and behind each low picket fence lolled young women with long legs, short skirts, and most friendly manners. They urged us to come in for a chat, but our leader was aiming for the fifth house along the block. As we turned in at that gate the friendly calls behind us turned to cat calls and coarse shouts.

In the house two women were all business. "Well, boys, who's first?" asked the elder of the pair. The doctor's son called out, "He is! And I'll come with you." Talk about a doublecross! He and the younger woman disappeared. All eyes focused on me. I blushed and gulped. To my incredible relief a nondescript dog wandered into the barren room and tapped across the grubby linoleum floor to where I stood in obvious panic. I patted his head. In different words the woman bawled, "Don't tell me you prefer my dog!" Before I could think of even a stupid reply the phone rang. She answered, hung up, and whirled on us, yelling, "Get out! It's the cops!"

With a mixture of blind relief and panic I dove for the rear of the house and fled down the back lane to the car parked on Fourth Street. There wasn't a police officer in sight, but the air was peppered with feminine laughter. Someone shrieked with glee, "We sure fixed her good! A hot night and she gets four! Oh yeah?" I knew where that phone call had come from. Bless her.

One thing for sure: it was no rascal bloody-handed beadle.

One-stop Shopping

HUGE GROCERY SUPERMARKETS ARE SPROUTing like springtime tulips, each better and, of course, bigger than its oversized neighbours. In my early days, we patronized the small corner grocery store–there seemed to be one at every suburban corner where the streetcar changed direction. But before they arrived on the scene, we did our grocery shopping twice weekly at John Irwin's grocery store on the south side of Eighth Avenue between Center and First Street West.

John Irwin was a large man whose ample waist was forever encased in a white apron. From behind a sizeable moustache he took the orders of the shoppers who faithfully patronized his business. He handled bulk items such as lentils, sugar, rice, flour, and biscuits, which were displayed in sloping bins with glass lids fronting the main counter. On the counter was a Fairbanks "Honest Weight, No Springs" scale, a fat horizontal roll of brown wrapping paper, and a nearby cone of cotton string. The string left its spool vertically until it reached a small set of well-spaced eyelets that led it back to the counter to be wrapped and knotted around the purchase.

You could count on Irwin to have whatever you needed in the line of groceries, be it raffia-wrapped earthenware jars of Oriental ginger in its own sticky syrup, glass-bottled guava jelly and tinned truffles from France, hot curried condiments from India, old country jams and jellies, Scottish marmalades, oatcakes, and shortbread, and English crumpets and baps.

One of Irwin's clerks was Henry Jenkins, who had been a potato sacker for his father in Mount Albion on Prince Edward Island. Henry decided to launch his own firm with another pioneer grocer, so they established themselves as Jenkins and Cornfoot at 1229 Ninth Avenue East, near today's zoo turnoff. Before the end of 1909, they had a staff of two clerks and two home delivery men, each with a horse and cart. A typical day's gross sales topped $420.

Henry Jenkins was an innovator. In 1914 he broke with tradition and hired female store clerks. He also visited Seattle to examine a merchandising scheme he had heard about. In 1918 he received a Dominion Charter giving him all Canadian rights and privileges to use Seattle merchant Walter Monsen's ideas and the name, Groceteria.

This was the Canadian start of the serve-yourself grocery store. By 1928 Henry's company had seven self-service Jenkins Groceteria retail outlets, a bakery, and a wholesale branch. Copycat newcomers were soon on the scene. Eaton's opened a self-serve grocery in 1925, in the Lancaster Building, four years before it built its Eighth Avenue department store. A U.S. chain with the unlikely name of Piggly Wiggly also appeared.

At the time of Henry Jenkins's death in 1945, his self-serve grocery business was thriving. The money-saving habit of shopping in person rather than phoning for home delivery had become part of a new way of life. Soon there were thirty-eight Jenkins Groceteria stores, of which seventeen were located in southern Alberta towns well beyond the edges of Calgary. Ultimately the firm consisted of forty-eight retail stores, a candy factory, and the wholesale grocery component. One of my old high school classmates, Ron Jenkins, followed in his father's footsteps and became head of the successful chain in 1950.

The last vestiges of the Jenkins empire, which had brought today's type of grocery shopping to this country, disappeared following Ron's death. The company's head office and cavernous warehouse occupied the old A.B. Cushing lumber mill property at Nineteenth Street and Ninth Avenue SE, less than a mile from the original two-horsepower home delivery store. The Jenkins and Cornfoot shop of 1909 bore a small ironic resemblance to today's supermarkets. Along with teas, jams, vegetables, and breakfast cereals, it carried wagon grease, buggy whips, and an assortment of horse remedies!

Facing page: The first Jenkins and Cornfoot grocery store opened on 1 July 1909. Seen here are the two proprietors, H.M. Jenkins and John Cornfoot, along with two of their clerks. *Courtesy Glenbow-Alberta Institute/NA-4501-2*

Batteries Not Included

WE ARE HEADED FOR HO-HO-HO TIME once again and the early toy catalogues are filled with incredible space machines that disintegrate a galaxy, trucks that crush any opposition, sub-surface instruments that cause deathly earthquakes, and creations for triggering cataclysms guaranteed to demolish the world and all who happen to be lollygagging around at the time. Of course "sets sold separately" and "batteries extra."

What a breathtaking prospect for already-harassed parents, and what an Armageddon for the little darlings whose damp curls frame beatific sleeping faces once they have been switched off for the night. While they are in the land of nod let's look back to a time when toys were a lot simpler yet every bit as exciting.

One of my all-time favourite Christmas gifts was a Sandy Andy. It was a triangular brightly enamelled creation consisting of a sloping track, at the top of which was a metal hopper. You set up the toy in a sandbox or a large roasting pan. If you kept the hopper filled with sand, the wheeled hopper car would tirelessly scoot up the incline, trip a switch to fill itself, then creep down the slope to dump its loads and scurry back for another batch. No batteries, no destructive inclinations.

One of nearly every boy's first playthings was an all-wood Tinkertoy. I am told it was invented seventy-some years ago by a stonemason who watched children playing with sticks, pencils, and empty wooden thread spools. Still basically the same, although plastics have been added, they tell me about a million sets are sold each year. Tinkertoy was a very new and exciting addition to the toybox when Santa gave me my first set. It surely must be the longest-lived of any of this century's playthings. Moreover, it is used by chemistry teachers to demonstrate molecular structures, as a skill test for new employees, and even in the designing of aircraft.

We lads "graduated" from Tinkertoy to Meccano. In those days the British-made metal toy came in an assortment of kits from beginner to expert. One set could be added to each increasingly complicated outfit. There were no colours, all were sturdy unpainted shiny metal perforated at precise intervals. It was possible, once one had outgrown the simple sets, to use a complex assortment of angles, corners, plates, braces, and links to assemble into buildings, robots, vessels, and vehicles. Each Meccano set, back then, included a generous supply of brass nuts and bolts and a small wrench, precision-made pulleys, shafts, and wheels. If Santa Claus could manage it in some later year, you might receive a Meccano clockwork motor to motivate your otherwise static creations.

My inventiveness led me to use an old twelve-volt auto horn motor. I mounted it on a board and, with the help of my electric train transformer, had it perform Meccano hauling and lifting jobs. It taught me torque and gearing, braking and stresses such as no Super Robot Dimensional Transitional Transposer could ever do—without a battery in sight. In those days clockwork power was vital, too. My first trains were clockwork, a bit unrealistic with their big key jutting out the side, but still capable of whirring a string of cars around an oval track leading to nowhere.

I had a clockwork army tank with an entirely new feature: it clacked as it clambered, spitting sparks from its forward gun. I remember having Father replace the flint that it needed for its lethal journeys. Another long-lived clockwork toy was a steamship. It trundled along the floor (no broadloom in those days) on tiny wheels at its keel. The key

The toys these Calgary youngsters received under the tree may have been simple—the finest things often are—but they brought endless happy hours to their young owners. *Courtesy Glenbow-Alberta Institute/NA-4630-4*

to wind up the mechanism was disguised as a plume of black smoke streaming from its funnel. I was still deeply fond of it when, in a fit of unplanned generosity, I gave it to my neighbour friend Billy Taylor, who was very ill and, until then, couldn't be soothed.

In those days there were friction toys, too. I see they are still alive and well in the newer toy catalogues. You revved them along the floor until their mysterious innards were really whirring, then released them and watched them tackle anything in their paths. Usually, acting terrified, they scuttled straight under a bed or down the cellar stairs or slammed into your mother's ankle.

Those were the days when girls' main toys were dolls with hand-painted china heads, real hair, and little china hands that grasped at empty air, their brightly painted lips parted in frozen ruby smiles. I remember my sister Mary's incredible joy the Christmas morning she found Joan under the tree. Joan could pose prettily on a metal stand and had the bluest eyes with real lashes. When placed on her back she promptly went to sleep, then popped back wide awake when set upright.

Mary, and some of the other girls on the block, had baby carriages, miniatures of the real thing, but complete with adjustable seat cushions and mattress and moveable fabric hood for protection against sun and weather. The wire-spoked wheels were always coveted by the nearest brother, who could envision them as wheels for his wooden lath T-stick with which he could outmanoeuvre other fast-running kids.

Girls' indoor pursuits back in the 1920s included cutting out coloured fashion models from Eaton's or Simpson's catalogues. Very carefully following the outline and remembering to leave little foldable tabs here and there, one could dress a basic model in any number of bright paper outfits.

Group pastimes of those days included board and dice games such as snakes and ladders, parcheesi, and ludo. One Christmas present was a realistic cardboard fish tank with cardboard fish, each with a tiny magnet. From your position at the side of the tank you tried to snag a fish with your bamboo pole, your success as an angler was determined by the number printed on the back of your fish. We played tiddlywinks, another game of long-lasting popularity. I believe it was invented in the mid-1800s and, thanks to celluloid (granddaddy of plastic) was still popular in my young days.

Checkers, dominoes, snap, and rook were other games, and we also built houses of old playing cards. We were even taught to play hearts and snap with cards, possibly placing us on the threshold, in later years, of learning adult card games such as five-hundred, whist, bezique, and, ultimately, bridge. But bridge and chess were far beyond my capabilities. Bridge entered my life many years later, but chess always baffled me right from my initial encounter with it at age thirteen. I really think mine is a Tinkertoy mind.

Perhaps that's why the modern Christmas assortment that includes Teenage Mutant Ninja Turtles, Pteranodon with Rasp Evil Warrior, Fearsome Flush, and Ankylosaurus with "Sting" Evil Rulon Warrior with full battle accessories frightens the heck out of me. I think I'll keep those "batteries extra" for my flashlight in case I begin, all over again, to get scared of the dark.

An Amiable Union

THE VILLAGE OF CRESCENT HEIGHTS GREW up alongside its older relative, the city of Calgary, for a few formative years, the two communities observing one another from either side of the Bow River quite unemotionally. However, the idea of union was flickering in the background, and in 1912 by means of a fairly simple annexation procedure, Crescent Heights was made part of the family.

The area had been crossed by the Morleyville Trail, which emerged from the mountains to the west. Crescent Heights was also important due to its excellent cattle-pasture land in the lee of the Spy Hill and Nose Hill ramparts on the north. For years, even when houses began dotting the prairie plateau above Calgary, cattle herds were driven along what today is Sixteenth Avenue, out of the foothills down today's Fourth Street East, to the stockyards. Once there they were assigned to eastern markets, to Burn's packing plant, or to ranch herds outside Calgary. For years, before it was designated Fourth Street NE, that drop to the river-bottom Langevin crossing was nicknamed Hay Hill because heavily loaded hay ricks on their way to the stockyards constantly "paved" the hill with slippery, spilled hay.

What really brought Crescent Heights (the North Hill is a generic term) into the Calgary fold was the completion of the Calgary Municipal Railway's track loop up the hill at Tenth Street at the west end, and Fourth Street at the east. The latter resulted in a couple of incidents that were exciting enough, though they did not capture the notoriety of the Fourteenth Street SW streetcar smash-up of 1919.

One snowy Sunday afternoon, a four-wheeled Tuxedo Park car defied its brakes and slid downhill towards the Langevin Bridge. Some of the passengers leaped to safety in adjacent snowbanks. The rest, who rode the runaway to the bottom, also escaped injury. Not so the small tramcar that only stopped when it caught up with, and bumped into, another of its own kind and size near the bottom of the hill, causing minor abrasions to both vehicles.

The other Fourth Street East mishap took place one weekday morning when a four-wheeler inbound from Tuxedo Park, loaded with office-workers, took the bit in its teeth on the hillside's curve, from where it jumped the rails, hit a pole, and flipped. About twenty Crescent Heights dwellers were hurt that time, mainly because of panic that developed when the car's overturned stove started a fire.

It was in 1911 that the street railway system extended the Tuxedo Park line from the Crescent Heights run, up First Street East, to loop at Twenty-ninth Avenue. Those were the days when people clamoured for a line running right past their house. Because of this, another large loop, called the Centre Street North, was added in 1919. The Capitol Hill feeder line came next, so North Hill residents were well served by streetcar routes.

This view of the North Hill prior to the 1920s shows how sparsely populated the area was at the time. *Courtesy Glenbow-Alberta Institute/NA-1604-24*

Crescent Heights itself was a fairly compact community but beyond it, after annexation, the area was peppered with new names indicating feverish speculative real estate development. Maps dated between 1912 and 1919 show communities named Houlton Gardens, LaGrange, LaHoyt, Clydesdale, Northalta, Ree Heights, the Bronx, the Golden Bronx, Knox Estate, Dundurn Park, Majestic View, and Richmond Hill—all competing to lure newcomers to buy and build on small groups of bleak, newly surveyed residential lots.

The village of Crescent Heights, at the time it was annexed, extended from the rim of the North Hill escarpment to Sixteenth Avenue on the north. From east to west it stretched between Twelfth Street NE and Twenty-fourth Street NW. One of the area's earliest households was the Chesney family. Mr. Chesney opened a hardware store on Sixteenth Avenue at Centre Street. One morning in May 1909, after a terrible three-day blizzard, a rancher found his lost, bewildered herd huddled around the Chesney store doorway.

Another early Crescent Heights family was that of Norman Cape, who used to pay the village $1.80 a year in taxes, an amount that remained static between 1899 and 1910. For years Norman Cape's wife ran the village post office located in W.S. Low's general store on Sixteenth at First Street NW. Norman's son John told me of going to classes at Balmoral, the handsome sandstone neighbourhood school designed by the eminent British town planner, Thomas Mawson. It was John Cape's uncle who erected the cast-iron clockless clock tower atop Balmoral School, fashioned by Irish-born blacksmith David Suitor's Calgary Iron Works. The tower—completed in 1914, except for the timepiece—dominated the Crescent Heights skyline.

Cape and his playmates often bundled up in winter to trudge in the snow to a very large frozen slough that lay on the bald-headed prairie not far from where the stately brick and sandstone Collegiate Gothic building (now Heritage Hall) arose to establish the dynasty we know as SAIT. That slough was a wintertime magnet for the children who lived in the central part of the North Hill.

The forty-four-and-one-half-hectare SAIT campus had been part of a big ranch owned by the family of pioneer settler Ezra Riley. It was Riley who donated Riley Park to the city. "The Tech," coupled with an improved Banff Trail (later the Trans-Canada Highway, then Highway #1A) began the North Hill's westward population drift. And back at its centre, in Crescent Heights, a fire station and horse team, brick offices and stores, and Calgary's first branch public library were established.

There is another interesting tidbit about that tower atop Balmoral School. One legend says the original four-faced clockwork arrived from its maker in Britain in an unserviceable condition. The manufacturer and the Calgary School Board could not agree on compensation, and certainly the board could not afford another purchase. A much more romantic story says the repaired clock mechanism was Canada-bound aboard the Titanic. You can forget about that one—the dates don't mesh. Another says the clockwork crisscrossed the Atlantic all through World War I as freighter ballast until it was too rusted for rehabilitation.

I like the story of the Coca-Cola salesman who, in vain, tried to convince people that the four blank faces, being white, should be back-lit to advertise in colour "the real thing." If the yarn is a true one, I applaud whoever vetoed the proposal. Crescent Heights, to my mind, has more classic roots than that.

Read All about It

EVEN BEFORE CALGARY OFFICIALLY BEcame a town, it had a newspaper. *The Calgary Herald, Mining and Ranche Advocate and General Advertiser* made its debut on 31 August 1883. Publishers Andrew M. Armour and Thomas B. Braden were farm boys from Ontario and had been friends since boyhood. Armour had a bit of newspaper printing experience before setting up shop on the frontier with his pal, a former schoolteacher in Peterborough.

They had the backing of Toronto milliner Frances Ann Chandler and an extra pair of hands courtesy of the local mounted police detachment, who loaned them Constable Thomas Clarke, a printer in civilian life. Their printing equipment had arrived on the first freight train to reach Calgary, addressed: "T.B. Braden, end of track." Before 1884 was over, they had moved their little business out of a tent into a shack and had hired Hugh St. Quentin Cayley as editor.

In 1885 Cayley, who had worked for the *New York Herald Tribune,* bought *The Herald.* Armour moved to Medicine Hat to start a newspaper, and Braden, who couldn't get on with Cayley, went to California where he and his wife became an evangelical team. Hugh Cayley stayed here and became notorious for his outspoken opinions.

One such "opinion" was that George B. Elliott, the publisher of a short-lived local rival paper, *The Nor'Wester,* was a childish egotist, a vampire, and a Lilliputian from nowhere! Cayley also took a round out of unpopular local Magistrate Jeremiah Travis, repeatedly calling him an arrogant eastern popinjay. That caper landed him in jail for a couple of weeks, but upon his release he was lionized by the small population, who staged a parade from the barracks to the newspaper office with celebratory stops at the saloons along the way.

In his absence another mounted policeman, G.E. Grogan, ran the paper, which, by then, Cayley had turned into a daily despite the limited number of readers. When a building and immigration boom in the early 1890s came to an abrupt end *The Herald* nearly vanished. In 1894 it was rescued by a bright young English newcomer, John J. Young, who brought it back to vigorous life.

For news, people bought *The Herald,* but for social comment and acerbic wit they bought Bob Edwards's *Calgary Eye-Opener*, which was published at irregular intervals! Edwards had brought his newspaper skills to Calgary via Wetaskiwin and High River.

The Herald's appearance was also a bit patchy. When Thomas Braden returned to work at the newspaper, Norman Luxton (who later founded the Banff Museum) was barely managing to keep it afloat. There was little money to pay bills such as those submitted by the telegraph service that supplied the news. In such cases Luxton would visit the railway station, read the papers carried through

The Hon. Hugh St. Quentin Cayley, 1891, was one of Calgary's first journalists, and was well known for speaking (or writing) what was on his mind. *Courtesy Glenbow-Alberta Institute/NA-795-5*

town by passengers, then nip back to get the latest into print.

In 1902 *The Herald* was doing well enough to afford the city's first two Linotype machines, which replaced the painstakingly slow job of setting type, a letter at a time, by hand. Back in its infancy in 1883, *The Herald* had complained in an editorial that mail took a month to travel to Calgary from Toronto. In those days the quickest route was by railroad in the United States to Fort Benton, then north by ox train to Calgary. Otherwise mail was sent to the end of the line as the CPR laid its trackage across the continent, and from there, with innumerable delays, had to wend its westward journey through the courtesy of whichever reliable soul was headed this way.

But once the railway reached Calgary it brought with it a fairly reliable telegraph circuit—an improvement in communication that encouraged further newspaper activity. The new kid on the block was *The Calgary News Telegram* (*The Nor'Wester* had disappeared by this time). Though *The News Telegram* had a short life-span, it made quite a splash. On Saturday 14 June 1913 it issued an eight-page "Prosperity Edition," the front page of which featured a lavishly imaginative bird's eye view of a mythical Calgary. That cover was even printed in black, golden brown, and scarlet!

An ornately coiffured woman is swathed in a cloak, her gown bearing a maple leaf brooch. She stands by a cornucopia on a Romanesque marble balcony gazing towards the distant Rockies beyond a skyline of spires, smoking chimneys, freight trains diplomatically labelled CPR, CNR, and GTP. Near a patch of unharvested fields and chunky office buildings stands a grain elevator and silo. A four-storey building bears the modest sign, "Nearly Everybody Reads the News Telegram." More than that, the woman holds at arm's length a copy of *The Calgary News Telegram* bearing a superimposed slogan, "A Great Newspaper in a Great City in a Great Country." This Freudian art work is attributed to the Calgary Engraving Company.

One of Calgary's remarkable newsmen, Fred Kennedy, worked for *The News Telegram*. Fred, an immigrant from Ireland, delivered papers at age twelve and was determined to become a news reporter. This determination had him delivering papers for *The Morning Albertan,* then gobbling breakfast at home in time to get to *The News Telegram* at 8 A.M. for an hour of clipping and filing duties. At 9 A.M. it was off to school, and when that was over, supper, then away again to *The News Telegram* where he did his homework, since it was quieter there than at home. Talk about dedication!

As the Great War raged on in Europe, wounded Alberta soldiers began arriving home. Young Fred, in an attempt to hone his reporting skills, spent much of his precious spare time at the railway station, scene of much news. He was given part-time jobs in the newspaper library and collecting photographs of Calgary war casualties from their next-of-kin. At the same time Kennedy was attending two night classes a week at Mount Royal College preparatory to taking entrance exams for the University of Alberta.

In 1916 Saskatoon newsman George M. Thompson bought *The News Telegram* and moved it into its own new building on Eighth Avenue West between First and Second streets West, opposite the Capitol Theatre. The presses were in the basement, visible to pedestrians through a row of large sidewalk-level windows. The editorial offices were at the top of a short flight of stairs on the raised main floor.

According to Fred Kennedy, publisher Thompson, "was red-headed and wore peg-top pants with a suit coat that reached almost to his knees. He also wore 'American type' boots with exaggerated toe swell, and smoked ill-smelling cigars. He had a large and pretentious private office complete with fireplace. His pride and joy was a huge brass cuspidor that he could hit dead centre with unerring accuracy."

Thompson renamed his afternoon daily newspaper *The Calgary Canadian*, and, in creating it, he inherited Fred Kennedy and managing editor Charles A. Hayden, who later became city editor of *The Calgary Daily Herald. The Calgary Canadian* lived only two years. As a parting gift, George Thompson solemnly presented Fred Kennedy with the giant cuspidor. Fred hadn't the heart to say he did not smoke or chew.

Charlie Hayden found a new berth as senior editor at *The Morning Albertan.* At the end of the war he had Fred join him there. For twenty-four years, Calgary's morning daily was owned and published by William McCartney Davidson, but *The Albertan*'s financial status didn't change. When Fred Kennedy was hired in 1919 he was told, "Your salary will be $14 a week, when you get it."

There were several other newspaper ventures over the years, not the least of which was *The Western Standard Illustrated Weekly*. I suspect the war scuttled that brave attempt, for the remnants of a copy I have bear the date Saturday 14 March 1914. It was a sixteen-page newsprint paper in two sections covering the topics of Financial and Insurance, Society, Sport, Business and Building, Motors and Motoring, Theatrical, and Late News. That was just the first section. In the second part were Within the Week and Other Stories, Editorial, Farming Page, Country Life, Women's Section, Stories, Prairie Provinces, and For Our Merchants.

Editor D. Matheson Sr. obviously felt that Calgary was well served with newspapers, for he busied himself tearing a strip off the Calgary Board of Trade for announcing that its secretary was going to publish a newspaper. He suggested that, "If the Board of Trade has so much money it does not know what to do with . . . it should hire a good, capable publicity agent to properly advertise Calgary and try and get some new industries." So there!

Clearly Calgary, even way back then, was a city with many loud opinionated voices.

Centre Street Guardians

YOU HAVEN'T LIVED IN CALGARY AS LONG as I have, so how could you possibly know? Know what? Why, that the four lions crouched on the Centre Street Bridge leap softly off their arched pedestals every midnight and head for Chinatown for a meal of, say, Szechwan beef, Yang Chow fried rice, and Kon Knam chicken while the rest of us are asleep.

How do I know this? Because my father, who was here long before the Centre Street Bridge was built, told me so, and he was a truthful man. At least, I think he was.

Let's see now, what else did he tell me about that queen of Calgary bridges? Well, for one thing, it was not the first one to span the Bow at that location. It seems that, despite the formidable sandy cliff on the top of which perched the village of Crescent Heights, Calgarians were determined to cross the Bow River at that very spot.

The nearest crossings at the time were far to the east and west. Up at Bow Marsh in 1884 a flimsy bridge linked the northwest corner of town with Cochrane and Morleyville and ranches to the west. Before long it was replaced, at a cost of $1500, by a sturdier wooden bridge financed by Eau Claire Lumber's Peter Prince. Downstream, in 1888, a new bridge on Dewdney Street (Fourth Street East) funded by the Northwest Territories Council provided access to and from the northeast corner of the settlement.

Back in 1882, there was a rowboat crossing known as Fogg's Ferry at Centre Street. Then, in 1911, a privately owned, steel toll bridge was flung across the stream. It was a rather lightweight affair but better than nothing. Of course, Felix McHugh, Philip Van Courtlandt, B. Godsal, and James Barwis, all farmers of riverbank land in the shadow of the cliff, were pleased to have such a permanent link with the town. But alas, permanent it was not. There was not nearly enough traffic to pay for its upkeep, and in its dilapidated state, was designated safe for pedestrians only for the final year of its brief life.

In their haste to span the river at Centre Street nobody thought to secure the Bow's permission, so it demolished the toll bridge at the first opportunity. It nearly destroyed a pair of city officials, too. City engineer George Craig, city commissioner John Garden, and an out-of-town visitor were examining the wobbly bridge during a vicious 1915 flood when the Bow took a swipe at the wooden approach at the north end. Before they knew what was happening, the three men were swept into the swirling waters.

Two city employees, Messrs. Powell and Garden, made their way in a punt to Garden and were able to tie a rope around him and tow him to safety. Meanwhile the police chief and fire chief and some others had raced downstream and fished Craig from the torrent near St. George's Island.

One of the four lions, sculpted in 1916, vigilantly "guarding" the Centre Street Bridge. *Courtesy Glenbow-Alberta Institute/NA-2399-91*

The visitor, unfortunately, drowned. So the Bow River, with its one-out-of-three-ain't-bad attitude, went back to harassing the bridge. In 1917, its dilapidated remains were sold to the provincial highway people for $1700.

Meanwhile Calgary City Council, in 1912, had sought the advice of Britain's foremost town planner, Thomas Mawson. He proposed another steel water-level bridge at Centre Street and to scale the escarpment at the north end, he suggested building a large elevator capable of lifting or lowering a load of two laden wagons, four horses, two drivers, and an assortment of pedestrians per trip. He anticipated heavy traffic–enough to keep elevator and bridge busy, and to pay all operating costs.

What a blessing nobody paid much attention, especially today's city traffic engineers who had to plan the reversible lane set-up now in operation.

Apparently the idea of a sophisticated river crossing had been suggested as early as 1913 during one of Calgary's boom periods. City engineer George Craig, city commissioner A.J. Samis, and Thomas Mawson all drew up plans. The public was to select one of the three designs by plebiscite. Ratepayers rebelled when the only plan they were shown was Craig's and flatly rejected the idea of a Centre Street Bridge as well as the $469,900 bylaw that would have financed it.

A few months later, miffed taxpayers notwithstanding, it was very apparent that a bridge was necessary. John F. Green, who later designed the concrete Mission and Louise Crossing bridges, submitted an acceptable plan. According to Bob Welin, ex-city engineer, past records reveal that because city hall in those day " . . . employed only one experienced draftsman, 'young ladies with artistic training and inclination' were advertised for and transferred the Engineer's plans onto working drawings." In November 1916 the present Centre Street Bridge was opened. The concrete structure took a year and a half to build and cost $375,000, a strain on civic coffers but well worth it.

The bridge was designed to clear the river by a good margin, although later floodwaters sometimes teased the lesser-known lower deck. The main upslope required carving a massive slice out of the Crescent Heights escarpment, a task undertaken by local contractor Ike Ruttle using horse teams and earth scoops aided by a steam-powered shovel.

The lions, apparently, were created by James L. Thomson, an immigrant Scottish stonemason employed by the city, and aided by a draftsman named Peter Borgesi. The "lion-building" was an international affair. Based upon Thomson's version of London's Trafalgar lions, the four concrete Centre Street beasts were rough-cast, then carved in a tent workshop set up in the shadow of the unfinished bridge. Two newly arrived Austrian brothers, Dymtro and William Stogryn, did the finishing work and were affectionately christened "Cement Joe" and "Cement Bill" by the bridge-builders.

Thomas Mawson would have approached his task in quite another way had he survived to see the tremendous traffic load carried by today's bridge. As for the lions, surely you'll agree they're a pretty spry seventy-two-year-old quartet? Although I wonder if they creak just a little bit as, at dawn with another Chinese meal in their concrete tummies, they crouch once again in their places to keep watch on traffic for yet another day.

Down t' the Deepo

WHEN THE CANADIAN PACIFIC RAILWAY threaded its way towards the mountains, this area was open prairie and river-bottom land. White settlement consisted of a missionary's tent and, shortly thereafter, the mounted police stronghold that became known as Fort Calgary.

The railway then plunked down a boxcar for a station. What annoyed the handful of tent and cabin dwellers was that the "station" was west, not east, of the Elbow River. But businesses and homes soon clustered around the new stopping place that marked the beginnings of central Calgary.

In the fledgling settlement, as in any small community, a favourite diversion was to "Go down t' the Deepo." You could stand close to the awesome heat, sounds, and smells of the steam locomotive, and watch the bustle as baggage was loaded and unloaded from the cars of the waiting train. Or you could simply do some people-watching as travellers came and went, or friends and loved ones parted from or rejoined one another.

The trains gave you the feeling of being in touch with the outside world. That was especially true when you pushed a letter through the mail slot on the side of the mobile post office—the mail car up at the front of the train.

It was easy to get within arm's length distance of the entire train at the CNR station. Its wooden platform stretched from Eighteenth Avenue to the railway bridge over the Bow. You could even stand beside the fireman with his long-necked oilcan as he squirted lubricant on the bearings, while the hot, panting locomotive appeared anxious to be on its way.

That station, originally St. Mary's sandstone community hall, was purchased for sixty thousand dollars in 1911 by the Canadian Northern Railway. In the days before it became the dead-end depot of a railway branch line to Calgary, St. Mary's hall had been rented to the Calgary Catholic school board for day and evening classes in arithmetic and English for immigrants. It was also the meeting place for the sixty-two-voice Calgary Operatic Society, a quaint thought now that the building, no longer a railway station, is a home to ballet in our city.

Much more auspicious was the occasion of going "Down t' the Deepo" when that meant the CPR sandstone railway station on Ninth Avenue and Centre Street. The last station to be located at street level, it was an important transportation hub for many decades following its opening in 1912. It was two storeys high, and its main trackside platform stretched almost two city blocks from the big rear bay window of the Palliser Hotel (on the site of a former small park and immigration building) east past a flower garden to the railway's six-storey Department of Natural Resources building adjoining the First Street East subway.

The station lobby was accessible from the

The CPR station, 1912. Visiting the hustle and bustle of the depot was always an adventure. *Courtesy Glenbow-Alberta Institute/NA-1451-36*

street through a row of heavy glass, oak, and brass doors. Between them and the avenue was a very large concrete apron and parking lot where an assortment of motorized tumbrel-like hotel buses were lined up. Their uniformed drivers shouted the amenities of each hostelry, hopeful of capturing the fancies of newly arrived passengers.

Within the station, the rotunda's white tiled floor bounced back the sounds of farewells and tears and the monotonous chanting of the train dispatcher. There were frequent arrivals and departures every day back then, with trainloads of people coming and going between here and Rocky Mountain House, Vancouver, Lomond, Edmonton, Acme, Montreal, Vulcan, and Halifax.

In the centre of the spacious main hall were contoured golden oak benches, worn shiny by years of waiting passengers and shelter-seeking loungers. On the east side of the lobby was a little news, candy, and tobacco shop at the mouth of a corridor leading eastward to the baggage office. The brass-barred ticket window on the west side was fronted by a brass rail to encourage the formation of a queue of ticket buyers. The clerk wore a green celluloid eye-shade and black satin sleeve protectors, almost a uniform. Behind him was a tall tiered rack of coloured tickets, banks of them ranging from little stubby cards for short train rides to shiny-paper "mile long" tickets to be dissected by successive train conductors as the journey progressed across the continent.

The dispatcher droned on about trains to and from Leduc, Raymond, the Crowsnest Pass, Banff, the Medicine Hat local that stopped at Cluny and Bassano, and the Lethbridge runs through Okotoks and on to where the two routes divided at Aldersyde.

On the trackside, or south, wall of the station, beyond another set of big doors, was a sort of "holding pen" of wrought iron with a single gate leading to the ground-level concrete platforms. The gate was presided over by an imperious, infinitely polite CPR policeman wearing an impeccable shiny-buttoned uniform and white gloves.

Whenever a transcontinental train rolled into the station, such as the Mountaineer, the Spokane Flyer, the Trans-Canada Limited, or the Dominion, it would arrive out of breath and ready for a window wash and an engine change, dead on time. In those days, punctual arrivals and departures of passengers trains were a matter of great pride.

After the arriving train had hissed and squealed to a stop, it occasionally had to be split by a fussy little yard engine, in order to allow access to a departing train on another track. Then, when all was clear and safe, the policeman opened the gate to allow travellers and friends to pour out to the trains and into waiting arms. Amidst the strings of passenger cars it was necessary to watch for signs and numbers identifying one's train and sleeping car. Black porters in snowy jackets, oxford-grey trousers, and gold-striped peaked caps helped the traveller and hoisted the baggage aboard.

Meanwhile stubby, tiny-wheeled, scarlet motor trucks beeped and chattered through the crowd towing strings of baggage carts, loads of fresh and soiled sleeping and dining car laundry, and ice blocks for drinking water and summertime air conditioning. The arrival of each long-distance train was the signal for a railway restaurant employee wearing a white bib apron to emerge from the station lunch room clanging a very loud brass hand-bell to announce that meals and snacks awaited the travellers' appetites during the twenty-minute stop.

The lunch rooms, strategically situated along

important rail routes, were immaculate but noisy because of the white tiled floors and walls, bare counters, and marble-topped tables. The Calgary lunch room served such consistently good low-cost meals that many senior members of the legal and business communities ate there regularly.

A short distance east of the station was the first stop, Maharg, at the junction of Eleventh Avenue and Twelfth Street East. It vanished shortly after 1912, having stood near the junction where the CPR lines veered north, south, and east. The north line's next halt was at Beddington, then Balzac, now almost within the city.

To the east, once clear of Maharg, the next stop was Ogden before the line headed onto the prairie and a stop at Shepard. Southbound trains halted at Turner Siding (today's Heritage Drive) before reaching Midnapore, well out into farm country. Regular and whistle stops were frequent as the train moved west. Along Spruce Cliff there was Critchley, Brickburn, and, opposite Bowness, the flag-stop (at Keith) Robertson.

For a very brief period during World War I, the Grand Trunk Railway station was located where Fort Calgary stands today. But it never did become the destination of travellers or a favourite haunt for those of us who loved to make an expedition of going "Down t' the Deepo."

Riding the Rails

THE C-TRAINS OF CALGARY'S YOUNG LRT system have some very important ancestors. Roots of the family tree were put down in 1907 by C.S. Lott, who imported three twenty-six-passenger motor buses from England. He called his firm the Calgary Car Company Limited and was proud of the fact that his were the first city buses in Canada. Only New York was ahead in this area, having introduced motor buses in 1905. Unfortunately the same problems faces by motorists for decades after that—mud, no proper roads, mechanical breakdowns, disgruntled customers—killed the enterprise within a year.

It was also in 1907 that Calgary City Council began administrative moves that would lead to the creation of the Calgary Electric Railway. One major challenge facing designers and builders of the street railway was the long and sometimes cruel winter. Another was the Calgary terrain with its two rivers, many creeks, deep and well-defined valleys, and growth potential, which promised to spread the city up, over, and out across the higher flatlands. This was enough to daunt the boldest transport expert.

City council's first move towards establishing a street railway was to pass Bylaw 740, which provided funding in the amount of $250,000. A track plan of belt lines was devised to minimize empty runs common to an "out and back" wheel-spoke layout. The deadline for completion of at least the first stretch of operating track was set at 1 July 1909. That is exactly the Thursday on which the first pair of trams began trundling with full loads of excited passengers between the Exhibition Grounds (Stampede Park) and the intersection of First Street West and Eighth Avenue.

The initial shopping list called for one sweeper, so a winter combatant was soon added to the little force to help service the year-round transportation needs of the scattered population of about thirty thousand. It was a four-wheeled sweeper identified as No.A, purchased from the Ottawa Car Manufacturing Company. It became one of the busiest vehicles on the system once the long cold winter of 1909-10 descended upon Calgary.

The vehicle was a double-ended wooden car equipped at each side with a small extensible pusher blade. An angular revolving brush of sturdy brown bristles sat ready at each end to clear the way. I remember myself and other pedestrians hunching—heads down, backs turned—while this rather impertinent little snow-sweeper passed by. Its brushes whirled outward and forward stirring every pebble and stone, flinging them hard enough to whap you quite harshly and endangering storefront glass along the road.

When blizzards hit, streetcars on outlying routes often stalled in snowdrifts until dug out by hand. At some unrecorded stage of its long life, sweeper No.A was converted to a single-broom

Calgary's streetcars served our city well for over forty years. This "two-man" streetcar was typical of those used when the Belt Line was in full two-way service, 1913. *(L–r)* R.G. Salloway, Walter Aarons. *Courtesy Glenbow-Alberta Institute/NA-1299-2*

and single-ended snow clearer. In 1920 the Calgary Municipal Railway acquired another similar single-broom four-wheeler from the same maker. Named No.D, it shared wintertime chores with the over-worked original.

Big-time help arrived eight years later with the purchase of Mary Ann, new flagship of the CMR's snow-fighting fleet. This was an eight-wheeled black monster with a tall multi-windowed cab, crowned by a reversible trolley-pole, and weighing in at about thirty-three tonnes.

Officially Mary Ann was No.H, a locomotive-type snow fighter armed with four angled rotary brushes and flanked by two long steel plough blades on either side. These could be retracted flat against the vehicle's sides, or extended like wings to scrape clear more than half the street at one pass. For twenty-two years, 1928 to 1950, she rumbled along Calgary streets whenever the snowfall warranted real muscle.

Motorists, seeing this majestic black battleship looming in the distance, took to the side roads while it passed. I remember it ponderously moving along Seventeenth Avenue West, clearing snow from curb to curb, followed by a line of cars—like birds riding above the white wake of an ocean liner.

A long-time friend, Frank "Scotty" Wilson, who worked for the Calgary Municipal Railway, had a fine collection of streetcar tales. One of his favourite stories occurred when he was motorman of a four-wheeled sweeper.

One winter night Scotty and his helper had completed sweeping the long, windy South Calgary circuit and were returning down the Fourteenth Street hill. With the bristly brooms whirling like frenzied curlers, the little four-wheeler began sliding. In the teeth of a blizzard, with visibility almost zero, they had no traction or control, and knew the peril of hitting cross-traffic at the intersection with Seventeenth Avenue.

With lights blazing and the power shut off, the two men flung themselves to the floor to ride the runaway to that great car-barn in the sky. Luckily they hurtled unscathed across Seventeenth, and, as the little tram slowed its pace, the pair clambered to their feet to peer through the storm. To their amazement they were still on the rails and had rolled to a halt just short of Twelfth Avenue.

On another winter evening Scotty was inching his eight-wheel Tuxedo Park car up the Centre Street hill. In deepening snow and facing a howling north wind, the car's wheels began to skid on the icy rails. Wilson set the speed regulator to its lowest notch and, corn broom in hand, stepped down from the creeping car out into the storm. He frantically swept the track in front of the grinding wheels, which, of course, began gripping the clean rails. The driverless car, with its passengers, began lurching up the hill.

Scotty flung his broom at the trolley pole as it passed him, hoping to cut the power by knocking it off the wire, but he missed. Soon the car wheels were spinning again as Scotty floundered in pursuit, and panting heavily, managed to scramble aboard, to the obvious relief of the somewhat apprehensive passengers.

Winterizing those streetcars was a work of art. They had storm windows, which added to the rattles, and a blower-driven coke stove and small fuel box immediately behind the motorman, making winter rides relatively cosy. At every car loop, when spring melted the snow, there was a cone of coke ashes beside the track where each driver had stopped to empty his brimming ash-pit.

Each tram carried a locally designed wrought iron "poker," freeing the driver from the icy task of leaving the warm car in inclement weather. It rested on a nearby hook, its lower end disappearing in a three-inch hole in the floor. One model consisted of a D-handle and a long straight shaft that ended in a broad, stubby blade. Another type had the head of a corn broom impaled on its shaft in place of the D-handle.

The streetcar was halted directly over a switch in the tracks while the motorman, using line of sight, lowered the gadget through the floor hole until its blade made contact with the switch. With a well-practised twist the switch could be snapped over, the poker withdrawn and hung up, and the journey resumed, all in the blink of an eye.

Thanks to persistence, ingenuity, and dedication, our Calgary Municipal Railway streetcars served us well throughout each winter for forty-one years.

Going for the Gold

THE STAGING OF THE XV OLYMPIC WINTER games was a proud moment in our city's history. We all have special memories of those triumphant days. For me in particular, the games provided new perspectives on what I used to call winter games when I was growing up here many decades ago.

You see, nuzzling one wall of the cottage on Twenty-eighth Street West, where we lived during my public school days, was a big oaken distillery-sized barrel. Rain water and melting snow from the roof of the little house was steered into it. My mother and sister, both with very long, tenderly cared-for hair, used the soft water collected there for shampooing. That is, until Father located two spare oak barrel staves and decided I should learn to ski.

In those days, skiing took place around Banff and was considered a rich man's sport–although I believe very few rich men had skis made of solid oak. So Father put clamps on the gently curved staves and left them soaking for weeks in the shampoo water barrel.

I understand completely the problems the Olympic skiing competitors experienced. They lost their hopes and balance and dignity the same way I did, not to mention some sponsor's shirt back home. Those barrel staves Father had liberated from a construction job in east Calgary never did work out. Happily, though, the ski venture cost our family no more than a half-dozen soft water shampoos.

I wasn't overly disappointed over that skiing fiasco. I was more of a scaredevil that a daredevil when it came to hurtling airborne on a couple of slats in the sharp wind of winter. That is why, in late November 1922, I was one of the fascinated and unenvious citizens standing comfortably winterized in the lee of the old Victoria Park grandstand.

Calgary was hosting the World Ski Jumping Championships that year as the climax to a winter carnival. The grandstand roof, which was about the size of a little aircraft carrier, had sprouted a high spidery jump of big timbers and a wood-decked run.

Competitors from all over the world gathered here and every one of them had to climb, complete with skis, up through the tiered rows of the grandstand seats, then through a roof trapdoor, out onto the roof, then finally up a ladder fastened to the side of the jumping tower.

After that immense climb they launched themselves down the big slope, into the air beyond the east wall of the building, soaring from there to ground level. That was the jump. Now how about the snow? Well, on 25 November 1922 the temperature stood at sixteen degrees Celsius, and over the next two days, went up to eighteen Celsius because a chinook wind refused to stop. In desperation the CPR was conscripted to fetch several trains of open gondola cars of snow from nearby Lake Louise. Fortunately, there was a siding to the fair-

The dual Riley Park toboggan run, 1920, provided Calgary children with their own "winter game" opportunities years ago. *Courtesy Glenbow-Alberta Institute/NA-1604-59*

grounds in those days but, even at that, it was an immense loading, speeding, unloading job by horse teams and sweating men. Loads of hay and straw used to cushion the landings helped slow down the melting.

The whole caper was a bit soggy and nobody recorded how many international backsides accumulated slivers and straw-burns. Still, the event was completed successfully, chuckled about, and well-remembered for years to come.

Now let's talk about that 1,480-metre bobsleigh and luge run. I have to admit that ours, even though it was built three or so miles closer to town, and sixty-two years earlier, was in a slightly different league. You might say it was reasonably priced since it only cost farmer Charlie Jackson a dozen or so dollars' worth of lumber, and an hour a week as he made the trip across his field with a horse pulling a barrel of water on a stoneboat.

You see, Charlie, a pillar of the Salvation Army and a terrific neighbour to us Killarney and Glengarry kids, had a hilltop field. It had a northeasterly drop that extended down through a grove of trees. Then it bore slightly to the left along a bit of a gully. As you emerged from the bottom of that, you had no choice but to make a sharp right turn because that was the CPR right-of-way. You were right alongside the tracks at the end of Tenth Avenue West.

Inside his property, on the bald crest, Mr. Jackson built an overgrown version of a school playground slide. At the start of a weekend when there were no classes at Sunalta School, he would slosh buckets of water on the wooden slope. By Saturday morning it would be frozen glassy-smooth, ideal for takeoff. You hauled your luge, bobsleigh, toboggan, whatever, up the ladder, flopped on your tummy and kicked yourself off down the slope. I'm told that's exactly what they did in 1988 out there west of town . . .

Those Olympic teams, it's said, hit something like 150 km/h on their multi-million dollar run. Heck, I bet I was doing at least 195 when I tried to go around both sides of a tree at once! Mind you, I had to be hauled home flatout on somebody else's sleigh in genuine agony. My Flexible Flyer with its scarlet runners and big varnished steering bar was demolished, as I nearly was. Bobsledding, luging, whatever, is not for the faint-hearted.

The next week I was back, though, with the Richardson kids who lived next door. Howard let me "borry a loan" of his old sleigh so that, back on Jackson's Hill, I could discover a better way of hurtling down through those trees. Mind you, the price of a new steering sleigh was too high for me to be given another one that winter, so I had to wait a whole year.

The following winter we had some breathtaking and, I suppose, less hazardous, runs down a (200-km/h?) double toboggan slope across town! At the top of the hill they were building a technical school we know today as SAIT. From up there, a wooden-framed side-by-side toboggan ran straight down that big hill, with no curvy stuff, and out and away across Riley Park until you scrunched to a stop in the snow.

Would it be permissible to say that, back then, judging by the "winter games" we kids held, we sure knew how to go for the cold?

Completing the Circle

CALGARIANS LOVE TO TELL VISITORS, DISAPpointed by the weather, to hang on a few minutes because it is bound to change. By the same token, I encourage young fellow-citizens to be as patient as possible, because just about everything "comes round again." I remind them that many unmapped prairie acres were accurately measured by the "rag wheel" method.

Having found a surveyor's mark a settler and his neighbour would measure the circumference of their wagon wheel. They would tie a rag on the rim, then set off across the wilderness, counting the number of times the rag completed a circuit. By multiplying the turns by the length of the wheel's rim they determined the length of their property lines. So, my parable dictates, if you wait long enough the wheel will complete a turn and, possibly, you will have covered some distance.

Newer and younger Calgarians, especially land developers, wax a trifle poetic over the precedent-breaking idea of building communities around man-made lakes such as Bonavista, Bonaventure, and Midnapore. One day back in the 1920s my father, in an especially reminiscent mood, drove me along a dusty trail far beyond the edge of Calgary, out near Shepard. There, at the edge of a field adjoining the road, sat a pair of desolate concrete gateposts. Beyond them were some derelict hunks of concrete that, in time, were hauled away to make room for crops.

Father explained that around 1910 a developer had the idea of scooping out some bald-headed prairie land and filling it with water. He launched his undertaking by encircling the as-yet dry bowl with a concrete balustrade punctuated by ornamental iron lamp standards that would illuminate the lake and the pedestrian promenade. Beyond the decorative edge of the lake he constructed a circular roadway, properly banked and ready for paving. As Father and I went through the gate he pointed out where he and his peers—young-bloods of Calgary with their newfangled automobiles—had raced around the uncompleted lake until the developer shooed away the forty-mile-an-hour speeding daredevils. Then, the treeless, unserviced residential lots unsold, and the electric railway line linking Chestermere with Calgary and a string of proposed communities along the route unrealized, the developer and his dream vanished.

Maps of 1912 show a northeast community named Albert Park. Set against the east side of the Fifth Meridian (Twenty-fourth Street or Barlow Trail), the area was bordered by Seventeenth and Tenth avenues on the north and south, and by Twenty-fourth and Twenty-eighth streets East. Its odd street layout can be explained by the centrepiece that was planned for the community seventy-six years ago—a triangular lake bordered by expensive homes in what became Forest Heights.

The complete circuit of the wheel pertains to

Motorists on the road between Banff and Calgary, 1913. *Courtesy Glenbow-Alberta Institute/NA-1497-36*

one of our highways, too. In 1909 an intrepid group of twenty-nine motorists—130 men and women—proved it was feasible to make the trip between Calgary and Banff. The struggle knocked out four cars and took a whole day to complete in each direction. But the venture opened up possibilities of linking the city and the town with a proper road rather than a prairie and woodland trail.

In the 1920s, in the face of entrenched provincial government indifference to tourism, local businessmen—including A.B. Claypool, MLA for Didsbury, and Calgary's Dan Whitney, owner of the Dominion hotel—created a company by the name of Trackways. The group asked the government for permission to build a twenty-four-foot-wide concrete toll-road between Calgary and Banff at a cost of $35,000 per mile.

The proposal, receiving absolutely no legislative encouragement, perished. However, it is worth noting that the route between here and Banff mapped by the Trackways Company forty years ago ran directly across country to the mountains on the south side of the Bow River. It took the better part of fifty years for this worthy idea to penetrate the ¼-inch skulls of the legislators. In the wake of years of "improvements" to the scenic but impractical old road we know as #1A, the Calgary-Banff highway has more than proved its worth.

Our magnificent downtown Devonian Gardens came very close to having an ancestor. In 1911 a young promoter named Bert Stringer, brother to Canadian author Arthur Stringer, burst onto the scene. Although born in Chatham, Ontario, Bert had spent very little time there. He had attended university in Cuba, and after graduating worked there for two years on a U.S. government engineering project.

Next, Stringer drifted around Central and South America and parts of the Orient and, somewhere along the road, caught malaria. He returned to Canada for a continent-spanning recuperative holiday by rail. When his train stopped in Calgary he fell in love with the place.

He dabbled in cattle, coal, then real estate with such success that he opened a branch land office in Calgary. He studied the market and, very shrewdly, bought the entire tract of farmland on which he created the district of Mount Pleasant. To improve access to it he linked his own enthusiasms with that of fellow developers. Together they lobbied successfully for construction of the fine new Centre Street Bridge that continues to rank foremost among Calgary's host of river crossings.

While the project was still in the planning stage, Bert Stringer's itchy feet took him to the Orient once again, this time to collect architectural ideas. His head loaded with schemes, he hurried back to his beloved Calgary and the handsome new turreted Mount Royal house he had built in 1911. (You can find it there today, on the southeast corner of Eighth Street and Royal Avenue.)

One of Stringer's newer downtown real estate purchases was a property on Eighth Avenue West adjoining the recently erected six-storey Leeson-Lineham Block. That tall, slim office building, bearing the name of the George K. Leeson and John Lineham partnership, attracted some prestigious business firms as tenants. It appealed to Stringer's commercial boosterism, for he could not resist indulging in a bit of "one-upmanship." He embarked on building a Calgary "first-of-its-kind" office tower.

The design called for a roof garden completely enclosed in glass, elegantly appointed, and lavishly endowed with exotic plants and flowers. The centrepiece would be a luxurious restaurant rivalling in quality and decor a tower dining room he had admired in San Francisco. Such opulence, such hyperbole, such schemes–typical of Bert A. Stringer, whose dreams and enthusiasms were ideal for fuelling the growth of the little city of Calgary.

The Changing Face of a City

A NEWCOMER TO CALGARY IN THE LATE 1970S said to me, "I love Calgary but when are they going to finish it?" Those were the days when cranes crowded the skyline as new office towers rose in the city's heart and columns of apartments reached for the suburban sky.

For a decade, when Calgary was exploding with new growth, no matter how familiar one was with the city it became a bit bewildering to return to a familiar place after a short absence to find that a building had vanished and preparations for a replacement were well underway. Recalling what had been on the site only a few weeks earlier was a challenge. Tougher still was remembering what had been on the site decades earlier.

How many recall the Ranchmen's Club, located in a rambling Seventh Avenue house surrounded by a spacious lawn and picket fence–the current address of the Bay Parkade and its shops? Parker's Department Store, bitter rival of the Hudson's Bay Company, sat at the west end of that block, its front doors facing The Bay across Seventh Avenue.

"Hotel Row," Fourth Avenue, was once a choice residential address. Its mansions were the centre of Calgary's wealthy society before the development of Mount Royal, and before a lawyer by the name of Lougheed and tycoons William Roper Hull, I.S.G. Van Wart, and Pat Burns, a meat packer, crossed the railway tracks to build their sandstone palaces on the Twelfth and Eleventh avenue prairie west of Fourth Street. Speaking of sandstone, in 1909 W.R. Hull erected the Grain Exchange Building on the site of the Chinese laundry where it is believed Calgary's smallpox outbreak of 1892 began.

Kitty-corner from that, the Palliser rose on the site of one of the prettiest downtown parks. The formal flower beds and pathways bordered by the station on the east, the tracks on the south, the First Street West level crossing to the west, and a Ninth Avenue livery stable, provided a riot of summertime colour and relaxation for wandering passengers while their trains paused for a few minutes in Calgary.

Two blocks east of the gardens was another local sandstone centre of considerable substance, the very busy Calgary YMCA, now the site of the Natural Resources Building. On Tenth Avenue West the Mount Royal apartment tower, which soars above the Palliser from across the tracks, stands where the railway's ice house and brick-chimneyed power plant and laundry used to be. In the downtown core the Lougheed Building at First and Sixth arose on land formerly occupied by sprawling Terrill's greenhouses, in earlier days a perfectly logical midtown business.

The block bordered by Eighth and Seventh avenues and Fourth and Fifth streets West always was a judicial one. A two-storey courthouse of rugged sandstone erected in 1885 faced east, as does its modern successor. It included the

Calgary's skyline in 1928. *Jack Peach Collection*

mounted police lock-up. A Paskapoo sandstone courthouse, built in 1915 to handle the increasing workload, faced Seventh Avenue; next door was the Land Titles Office, with Calgary's first museum housed in its basement.

The Stephen Avenue Mall intersection with Second Street West has undergone major changes over the years. The W.R. Brock dry-goods wholesale warehouse sat on the southeast corner in the days when that was well out towards the west edge of the business district. Across Second Street was Head's locksmith shop, replaced by the Canada Life Assurance headquarters, now called the Hollinsworth Building.

Former Mayor J.S. Mackie captured nearly all the grain companies as tenants when he erected the Lancaster Building, one of our town's early skyscrapers. The Frontier stable, owned by R.C. Thomas, was the first occupant of that intersection's northeast corner. Thomas later replaced his horse barn with the Royal Hotel. It was inevitable that Calgary's expansion frenzy would eyeball that hotel and the Webster Block behind it, which housed oil offices as well as additional hotel rooms, to round out the Scotia Centre site.

That lofty building rises today where, for years, the United Cigar Store occupied a small piece of the hotel corner. The Lancaster also spreads across the old location of the Capitol Theatre, our most impressive and luxurious picture house, that faced Eighth Avenue and reached through the depth of the block because of a flyover crossing the back lane.

Where Eighth Avenue and Fourth Street meet

Calgary's skyline in 1979. *Courtesy Glenbow-Alberta Institute/NA-3105-1*

a streetcar-like diner once angled across the southwest corner, diagonally opposite Eaton's, having been moved a block west from its original Eighth Avenue site. Next to it, near the subway, was a telephone building. Adjoining it on Eighth—today's Penny Lane—was a row of warehouses that were later converted into the Colonel Belcher Hospital.

One of the most startling replacements is the soaring Bank of Montreal tower on Seventh Avenue and Third Street West. I wonder how many people remember when it was the two-storey brick Fisk Tire store. Across the lane immediately north of it on Third, stood the Medical-Dental Building with its brick and stone facing. The stone portion, at ground level, revealed the fossilized remains of trilobites and other marine creatures from the seas that covered western Canada millions of years before the cranes temporarily nested atop Calgary's new towers.

Remember when Calgary had one liquor store? It was at 330 Ninth Avenue West, having replaced a wholesale food produce warehouse. As the city grew, the number of liquor outlets increased, and the building became petroleum company head offices with a giant revolving neon "66" hawking gasoline from its roof. And who would believe that Calgary's largest shopping complex covers acres on the west side of the Macleod Trail where, thirty-nine years ago, stood the Chinook Drive-in Theatre?

In your travels around Calgary keep an up-to-date map handy. As things start to pick up again, you may get lost when someone replaces a homely landmark with another cloud-grabbing tower.

On the Way to Nowhere

WE ALL HAVE SPECIAL CHILDHOOD MEMOries we love to retrieve from the cobwebs of our minds and savour now and again. Those of you who grew up in Calgary many years ago may recall some of these.

For example, Ingraham's Shoe Store, on Eighth Avenue near Third Street, was the first to have one of those X-ray machines that would drive some of today's twittery mothers into a frenzy. Lanky George Ingraham would have you take off your scuffed and worn shoes while your mother, sitting beside you, hoped you had not put a hole in your sock on the trip to town. He would slip on a new pair of shoes, then instruct you to stand very still on the low platform of a contraption resembling a weighing machine, with your feet well forward in a sort of slot.

Mr. Ingraham would flip a switch and have you peer through a rubber-rimmed viewing glass. Down there, bathed in a green glow, were your feet, all bones, encased in new shoes. "Wiggle your toes," he would urge so you did and, lo, your green bony toes would wave up at you.

There were special eye-pieces, one for him, the other for Mother to look through. With their eyes glued to the unfolding drama they would nod and mutter sagely while you proved, by wiggling, that there was lots of room in the new shoes. That is, until you grew enough to crowd your toes as tightly as you had in the old pair. So Mother and Mr. Ingraham would prescribe the next size larger in which your feet sloshed about until they grew or the shoes wore out, whichever came first.

Speaking of firsts, fun in the river topped the list of our summer favourites. In the late 1920s the city diminished the risk of swimming in the Elbow by stringing telephone poles end-to-end across the stream at the top and bottom end of a stretch of river near Thirtieth Avenue and Elbow Drive (called Sixth Street in those days). That part of the Elbow had a sandy bottom so it became a very popular swimming place. An open lawn was planted between the Elbow Park streetcar track and the water just below the Freddie Lowes house—perfect for sprawling on after your swim.

Youngsters were under the watchful eyes of older kids, and everyone was warned to keep to the stretch of water between the pole "barriers." It was not very deep during the warm weather; but because it was still a running river with a current and the occasional deep spot, we learned to respect it and not take chances.

Downstream from that swimming place, out behind the Holy Cross Hospital and the CN Station, was a really exciting swimming hole. The old tree that leans over the stream has been used by generations of kids as a rope swing. You'd scramble up the bank, grab the dangling rope-end, and swoop out over the deepest part of the river, then let go. That always has been a real old-fashioned

Swimming in the Elbow River (off Elbow Drive) topped the list of favourite summer activities for Calgary youngsters in days gone by. *Courtesy Glenbow-Alberta Institute/NA-4099-12*

"swimmin' hole" despite nervous parents, aldermen, and mayors, who at one time or another have all urged that the practice be stopped. Had they succeeded they would have eliminated one of the great joys of being young.

The only spot in the Bow those of us from the south side of town swam in was a lagoon behind Lowry's Gardens at the east end of Spruce Cliff. It was best suited to splashing rather than swimming, but it was a sun-drenched backwater. The Lowrys, always silently busy in their market garden, paid us no heed. Spruce Cliff was a wilderness of evergreens, and the only sounds of life came from across the river where we could hear the Bowness streetcar clanked its way through Parkdale hourly.

The mouth of the backwater was beside the CPR main line, at the foot of the cliff. We were what you would now call skinny-dipping, but back then our clothes piled at the water's edge proved we were swimming "bare-nekkid." When someone hollered that a passenger train was about to roll by we'd stand ankle-deep, like jay-birds, and wave at the passengers we smugly believed were shocked out of their very seats.

We would often bicycle along Killarney's dirt roads and out across the open prairie to Spruce Cliff. On the steep, fragrant hillside we had favourite paths and perches where we would squat in the cool of the afternoon, watching golfers on the brown parched fairways of St. Andrew's Golf Course. Then, below us, the arm of the semaphore signal beside the track would point skyward giving the "all-clear" to an approaching eastbound train panting smokily from its long trip across the mountains.

From our eagle's perch we could almost peer down the hot smokestack of the locomotive as it prepared to slow down through Sunalta and roll to a stop beside the Palliser Hotel. As the thunder of the train faded to the east, the striped signal arm would drop as though to block the way. That meant no more trains were due to pass so we would head back up the cliff and home.

Another long-gone sight and sound we enjoyed as youngsters was the activity of Oliver's Quarry. You could not find it today, because its remnants lie well-buried beneath the Crowchild Trail's uphill slope between the river and South Calgary. That cleft was a treasure-trove of sandstone, sort of the birthplace of many Calgary buildings including City Hall.

From the gassy hillside above the west side of the quarry we could look down as big blocks of sandstone were pried loose and eased to the quarry floor. There, a boom crane built of husky wooden beams shifted them into position to be sawn and shaped. A small coal-fired steam donkey-engine supplied the power, although I still remember the sympathy I felt for a pair of horses whose dreary job it was to plod in a circle to operate a windlass.

High above the quarry floor, an earthen causeway carried the Killarney streetcars along a single line beside a narrow gravelled road. It was a flimsy-looking approach to sparsely settled Glengarry and Killarney and the scattering of houses that dotted the prairie out towards Rosscarrock and the power line. Bored from watching the heavy pace of work down in the quarry and knowing no streetcar would obligingly topple off the spindly roadway of Seventeenth Avenue, we sought more stimulating sights and sounds.

On the way to nowhere in particular sometimes we settled for a chance to peer into Mr. Keen's tiny shop on Twenty-third Avenue, where the short, stout shoemaker would set his wheels and brushes spinning just for us. We admired the way he skilfully trimmed the soles and heels of a new pair of shoes.

As kids we certainly indulged in the usual quota of youthful mischief; but looking back on all this I readily admit that life seemed much simpler then. Don't you?

The Midas Touch

MANY PIONEER CALGARIANS ARRIVED HERE on horseback or on foot plodding westward alongside their teams across the bumpy prairie grassland. A notable exception was William Roper Hull, who made his way here from the west with a herd of twelve hundred horses in 1883.

Hull and his brother, John, were vigorous teenagers from the west of England who, in 1873, set sail for the new world. Their ship brought them to Panama, where a canal was under construction to link the Atlantic and Pacific oceans. The Hull brothers, too impatient to await the day ships could navigate the sixty-four-kilometre canal, set out on foot across the Isthmus of Panama to find passage on a northbound ship on the Pacific Ocean.

They sailed for Victoria via San Francisco, then made their way across to the mainland and up the Fraser River by steamer and stage coach. Before long, they were firmly established as horse ranchers in the hilly grasslands of the Kamloops area. Hard work and good fortune made it possible for W.R. and J.R. to assemble twelve hundred head of horses and set off for a prairie market they had heard was hungry for horses. They drove the herd through the wilderness of the Crowsnest Pass and the foothills, up to Calgary, where they sold the horses to the mounted police and the Northwest Cattle Company.

William Roper Hull sensed this was the place to make his fortune. Over the next three years the Hull brothers landed a big contract with the Canadian Pacific Railway to supply fresh beef to construction crews in British Columbia. In 1886, from their Kamloops spread, the brothers organized another livestock drive to the prairie with three thousand head of cattle and five hundred horses.

To ensure their position as suppliers, they sold only two-thirds of the stock, pasturing one-third on spreads they bought at Pine Coulee west of Nanton, and on their six-thousand-acre Oxley Ranch in the Porcupine Hills, where they soon had eight thousand head of cattle and two hundred saddle and workhorses. For his home base and feed source, William Hull bought fifty-three hundred acres, which he operated as a model grain farm close by the junction of the Bow River and Fish Creek. One of his many claims to fame was that of being the first large-scale shipper of livestock by rail once the CPR link had been completed between Kamloops and Calgary.

Hull continued into the early 1900s to raise and sell about two thousand head of cattle and three hundred of horses annually. On the Fish Creek spread, widely known as "the old Government farm," he experimented with irrigation that, to his great satisfaction, noticeably improved the yield of oats, barley, and wheat. This trial activity led W.R. into bankrolling the Calgary Irrigation Company, a pioneer in its field.

Although the idea of living in nearby Calgary appealed to him, he decided to remain on the Fish Creek property. There, Hull built a lavishly appointed $12,000 mansion for himself and his wife, Emme (Emmeline Mary), who was described to me by Calgary old-timer Gordon Cummings as "a sweet and always cheerful woman." While still a rural resident, and not a dedicated follower of the lively arts, Hull nonetheless felt a theatre was an essential part of any community. So, in 1893, he presented Calgary with Hull's Opera House, a one-thousand-seat, $10,000, two-storey sandstone theatre that could accommodate one-quarter of Calgary's population. Up to that point Boynton Hall had been the only, though very inadequate, venue for concerts and social gatherings. For the next thirteen years Hull's Opera House was the focal point of Calgary's cultural life. It was lavishly endowed with three tiers of seats in a horse-shoe formation, a soaring arched ceiling, and a generous stage that projected well out into the crowd, providing performers with an agreeable intimacy with their audiences.

Competition from newer

William Roper Hull was a prominent Calgary citizen and businessman when this photograph was taken in the early 1900s. *Courtesy Glenbow-Alberta Institute/NA-514-1*

theatres ended the show business career of the opera house in 1906. Meanwhile, in 1902, W.R. and Emme moved into the Calgary where they had built another lavish mansion. It stood on Twelfth Avenue and Sixth Street West opposite today's Ranchmen's Club. In fact, it backed onto the big new sandstone home of Pat Burns. A few years earlier, in 1896, Hull had sold the British Columbia portion of their meat business to his brother John. Then, in 1904, W.R. sold his Alberta meat business, his Fish Creek mansion, and many of his land holdings to his meatpacker neighbour Burns, in order to concentrate on his many other investments. This meant the brothers had divested themselves of fifteen northwest Canadian branch outlets for their meat products.

To fill that gap, as it were, William Hull plunged with great success into the real estate and investment business. At one time he owned valuable properties in Victoria, Edmonton, Calgary, Lethbridge, and Medicine Hat. Among the downtown structures he built was his own office, the Hull Block, on the southwest corner of Eighth Avenue and Centre Street, complete with clock tower and curved front glass windows. It later became the headquarters of Burns and Company and soon bore the Burns name.

W.R. Hull was a man with a Midas touch for real estate and his commercial investments and undertakings were very successful.

In 1893 Hull, A.E. Cross, and Senator Matthew Cochrane organized the Calgary Brewing and Malting Company, boasted to be the most modern and complete brewery in Canada. Hull and Cross were financial buddies who successfully parlayed one investment after another. Metals Limited, a most successful wholesaler and distributor of metal components for homes and businesses, of which Hull was president, was one of them. He kept his hand in ranchland property, at one time owning two spreads, the Beaver Camp Ranch in the Willow Creek area south of Pekisko, and the Sheep Camp Ranch north of Calgary.

Although Hull built several midtown structures, the six-storey Grain Exchange Building, a skyscraper in its day, stands out as a venerable pillar of his "Calgary empire." Built in 1909, it was expected to help wrest the grain trade from Winnipeg. Brokers eagerly rented big-windowed and oak-trimmed offices in this newest and tallest building in Calgary. It was a brave attempt, but World War I and the Depression caused the grain men to break ranks, moving to the newer and more imposing Lancaster Building and the Lougheed Block.

Mrs. Hull lived at Langmore, as they called their Twelfth Avenue home, for twenty-eight years following her husband's death in 1925. The Hulls were childless, but in W.R.'s will were bequests for relatives. Upon their demise, long-term provisions made possible the founding, in 1962, of the William Roper Hull Home with three-quarters of his remaining fortune. In place of the children he never had, abandoned and troubled youngsters were sheltered and raised there at his estate's expense. Now, with a broader mandate, the facility is called The William Roper Hull Child and Family Services, with nearly one hundred young people in its care, providing child and parental therapy and consultative services.

William Roper Hull left a very large footprint upon our local landscape. His contributions were recognized formally a few years ago when he was honoured by federal historic authorities as "A Person of National Historic Significance." It was a well-deserved honour.

Now That Was Service

WHEN CALGARY WAS ABOUT THE SIZE OF today's city of Lethbridge, nobody lived very far from the heart of downtown's commercial establishments. The few communities located on the flatland beyond the centre bowl of Calgary had a scattering of neighbourhood stores. So, for those who wanted it, most businesses maintained a horse and wagon or, at least, bicycle delivery service.

Daily home delivery was the rule rather than the exception, milk distribution being typical and, laudably, still available. The Carlyle Dairy Company was established in 1909 at 220 Fifth Avenue SE by brothers J.W. and T.M. Carlyle. "Quality and Cleanliness" was their motto, emblazoned on their delivery wagons, which trundled daily from the three-storey brick dairy. Their four-wheeled carts, white with gold lettering, each pulled by a sleek horse, were seen in every part of the city from midtown restaurants to the scattered homes of outlying residential streets.

The sides of the topless wagons reached thigh-high on the standing driver. Lining the aisle to the rear steps were bins where glass bottles clinked amid chopped ice, which kept the butter, milk, buttermilk, eggs, and cream fresh and cool. In winter the ice was replaced by blankets to ensure that products did not freeze. The driver's sole salvation from winter's cold and summer's rain was to keep moving briskly along the tedious house-to-house route.

Usually the horse knew the route as accurately as its driver, so the two often appeared to meet almost casually when the milkman had to drop off empties and refill his metal basket. This "horse sense" was especially useful at Christmastime when the thoroughly chilled driver was tempted throughout the route by excessive customer hospitality.

Our bakery delivery man in Elbow Park was a ramrod-backed ex-British Army sergeant major with a ruddy face and steely blue eyes who had known years of brilliant sunshine in northern India. As he mounted our back steps he would sing out, "Bay-kahh—Goood Maw-ninnggg!" then stand at the door with his wicker basket loaded with bread, cakes, and buns. His roofed wagon was polished and bore the "Shelley's 4-X Bread" insignia. His handsomely groomed horse wore brass-studded blinkers and other horse brasses on its harness.

By the driver's feet was a nosebag of oats for the horse's lunch, and, on the end of a long leather line, an iron tether-block or halter-weight to keep the animal from drifting when the driver was busy with customers. Back then, scattered around the business area of Calgary, were curbside concrete troughs of fresh running water to slake the thirst of the hard-working horses.

In the early years of this century businesses large and small had their own delivery horse rigs. The Hudson's Bay wagons were a stirring sight. Enamelled in the company colours of dark green,

Horses were essential to the frontier. In Calgary, in addition to day-to-day delivery of groceries and drugstore items, horses were a vital part of fire brigade rigs such as those pictured here at #2 Fire Station, 1905. *Courtesy Glenbow-Alberta Institute/NA-9673*

gold, and black, they rumbled behind pairs of matched draft horses. In time they were replaced by a fleet of trucks. Burns and Company hauled its meat in big scarlet and gold wagons pulled by teams of greys, each driver and swamper dressed in uniform cap, gauntlets, and white dust coat. The Swift Canadian Company added somewhat similar colour and formality to Calgary's downtown traffic.

The Ontario Laundry, operated by the three Christie brothers, had fifteen teams and wagons that fanned out from their laundering and dry-cleaning plant at 302 Fifth Avenue East. In the days before Mother had a washing machine, she would bundle the week's laundry into a bed sheet, knot it, and hand it to the delivery man in exchange for last week's completed wash-and-clean job.

Calgary used to have a number of cartage companies such as Elk Livery at 319 Sixth Avenue, run by Ike Ruttle and Fred Birmingham. They specialized in business and residential delivery and baggage transfer, such as fetching steamer trucks and suitcases from the railway stations to destinations throughout town. A rival firm, in addition to the railways' own baggage and cartage services, was Calgary City Delivery. Their Tenth Avenue East warehouse and offices backed onto one of several railway spur lines that penetrated some of our midtown back lanes. They kept their sprawling business humming with eleven transfer wagons and horses hastening about the city with everything from parcels to railway carload lots.

Even little firms such as the neighbourhood Sunalta Grocery gave its customers free door-to-door delivery, with the proprietor himself driving the rig while his wife "minded the store." In those days, about 1912, the Inglewood area sported a cluster of grocery, butcher, and provisions shops. Along Ninth Avenue East were the grocery firms of Summers at 1208, Jenkins and Cornfoot at 1229, Frizzle at 1316, and People's Meat Market at 1325. All but one had a pair of horse-drawn rigs for delivering food orders to customers. The only possible example of one-upmanship was that grocer R.J. Frizzle had three delivery wagons!

Wiggins & Co., whose grocery, meat marketing, and small hardware firm was located on Fourth Street at First Avenue (across the Bow in Riverside) had a pair of wagons, as did the Sunnyside Meat Market over on Tenth Street NW. A pair of four-wheeled one-horse rigs apparently were within comfortable economic reach of small businesses. In those days the costs and the distances were such that no extra charge was made for such personalized service. The majority of shops delivered. Drugstores, whose orders might be no larger than a single bottle of patent medicine, depended upon the pedal power of reliable neighbourhood cyclists—lads with a hunger for pocket money.

In the big league of horse-powered dray delivery were the railways' baggage transfer and freight haulers, and such local firms as Our Own Delivery Service established about 1910 by L. Richards, who had been a pharmacist's clerk before coming to Calgary and starting his own business. He undertook to transport everything from furniture to baggage and office documents, almost a glorified version of today's couriers. Richards was a trendsetter, for not only did he use seven horse-drawn delivery wagons, he took the bold step in 1912 of adding a motor delivery truck to his fleet.

The responsible job of distributing ice, in those pre-electric refrigeration days, was handled by Frederick Arthur Johnston's twin activities, Johnston Storage and Cartage Company founded in 1907, and the 1910 Arctic Ice Company. The diversity of his undertakings required that he maintain sixteen horse teams and heavy wagons for freight hauling machinery, plate glass, security safes, and furniture. Additionally, five pairs of horses trundled blocks of ice around the little city to business and domestic customers. Johnston's head offices were on Ninth Avenue East conveniently opposite the CPR freight sheds.

Throughout the 1920s and most of the 1930s horse-drawn wagons, drays, and carts continued to clip-clop around the centre of town and through the suburbs. But, as labour, fuel, licensing and stable costs rose, it spelled the end of universal home delivery and the once-familiar sights and sounds disappeared from the streets of our city.

A Busy Corner

*F*OR YEARS WE CALLED IT THE ALBERTA CORNER, and often identified this spot as the place to meet friends and appointments. To this day the corner bears the address of 804 First Street West, and is identified in the telephone book as The Alberta Block. If you stand across the mall from it, you will see a well-preserved, third-storey stone carved with the words "Lee and Brealey Block, 1888." It took the pair from 1888 to 1890 to complete the building.

It was the sandstone Alberta Hotel, sharing corners of the intersection with three banks and its hospitality with a host of early Calgary characters. Historian William McLennan, in his book *Bed and Breakfast: A History of Hostelries and Eating Establishments in the Area of Calgary* (1989), writes of the opening of the building:

> At 8 P.M. on January 18th of 1890 a pretentious 'citizens' dinner was held to formally open the new Alberta Hotel.
>
> Included in the fifty-seven guests who sat down at one long table were: Mayor Lafferty, Messrs. Hull, Rouleau, and Marsh, and Mrs. Lougheed. Mayor Lafferty spoke on Calgary's history and also spoke warmly on the enterprise of Lee and Brealey in erecting so commodious and well equipped a building. Mr. Marsh told how he had purchased all the lots on that part of the block, and that he sold the corner lots on condition that a hotel would be built on them. The hotel owners had paid Marsh five thousand dollars for the property. Following the dinner there was dancing from 10:30 until 11:45.

For several years the Alberta Hotel, under the skilled management of Henry A. Perley, was the finest hostelry between Winnipeg and Vancouver. The Perley family roots were deeply planted in the St. John River valley of New Brunswick, Henry's great grandfather having been sent by the governor of Massachusetts in 1760 to colonize the valley. Henry's own background was in farming, then running boarding camps for the Canadian Pacific Railway as it threaded its way westward. It was a natural progression for Perley to enter the hotel trade, and he ran successful prairie hostelries in several western towns along the new line.

For ten years Henry Perley managed the CPR's Glacier House at the west portal of the Connaught Tunnel, and was the first manager of the railway's Revelstoke Hotel, which opened in 1897. When the Alberta Hotel was completed in 1897 Perley leased it and, within a few years, moved here to spend the next fifteen years as its proprietor. Henry Perley died in Calgary in 1933. Although he was buried in California, locale of his wintertime retirement, Calgary was his home. He willed his money to our General Hospital to finance the Perley Wing.

The Alberta Hotel on the southeast corner of First Street West and Eighth Avenue. Erected in 1888, it was one of the finest sandstone structures of its day and was a popular meeting place for Calgarians. *Courtesy Glenbow-Alberta Institute/NA-205-2*

The second and third floors of Perley's hotel were in the shape of a hollow rectangle meaning that some rooms had an "inside view." On the main floor the lobby was furnished with overstuffed black leather sofas and chairs and the adjoining dining room accommodated forty-eight mealtime guests at half a dozen eight-place tables. Oriental waiters, linen table cloths, sturdy silver-plated tableware, and a well-endowed menu made it a popular rendezvous in the little city.

The dining room had a truly frontier presence featuring elegantly served dishes. The Christmas 1913 menu included: Loin of Bear Cub Casserole, Breast of Mallard Duck, Larded Rump of Moose with Mushrooms, Venison Steak Chasseur, and Planked Moose Tenderloin, along with Dungeness Crab, Kenniwich Salmon Steak, English Sole, Suckling Pig, Prime Beef au jus, and Turkey Newburg.

The Alberta Hotel bar was very popular. Although it did not have the west's longest bar as some would have you believe, its thirty-five-metre length and its business volume often required the services of ten barmen.

A regular visitor to the Alberta Hotel's assorted amenities was "Deafie" Wilson. He may have been a little hard of hearing, but J.J. Wilson, an early

Calgary architect, used his impairment, if any, to good effect. According to my father, "Deafie," everyone's friend, would hang around the Alberta Hotel bar waiting for someone to open a conversation. No matter what remark was addressed to him, Wilson, pretending not to understand, invariably replied, "Thanks, I don't mind if I do!" thus earning himself a steady supply of donated drinks.

Alberta Hotel barman Tom Pierce made the news as a result of a lone holdup attempt. Confronted with a gun, Tom calmly armed himself with a soda water syphon and whipped it from under the bar, skilfully pointing it between the thug's eyes. His aim was true, the surprise complete, and the gunman fled empty-handed. One of my acquaintances many years ago was Bill Conrod, a founding member of the Alberta Hotel Association and, for years, a night clerk at the Alberta Hotel. Bill was the hotel's first accountant and one of his achievements was to converse quite well in Chinese, something he learned from the dining room staff. At the youthful age of twenty-two he also learned much about life from the regular patrons of the hotel such as newspaperman Bob Edwards, and two of the Big Four stampede fame, Pat Burns and George Lane, both of whom lived at the 120-room hotel.

Bill Conrod, in his ninety-first year, told me stories of Gray, the hefty hotel chef they nicknamed "Bony" because of his great size; of head porter Fred Birdie and chief clerk Ted Shelley. He said that one table in the hotel dining room was reserved for Richard Bedford Bennett and his cronies. Whether "R.B." was present at mealtime or not, nobody was permitted to sit at his table even though the dining room was otherwise filled to capacity.

Bill told me, too, that at one time there was upstairs indoor access to the hotel's neighbour, the Royal Bank, so the hotel enjoyed reciprocal spin-off business with its adjoining business firm. A couple of other amenities made the Alberta Hotel popular among the local people. It had two basement bathrooms where a dusty cowboy could scrub himself for fifty cents, and a twelve-chair barbershop run by Charlie Traunweiser (later a hotelier in his own right) where businessmen could get a trim, and gossip with such barbers as Charlie and Jack Rose and George Benedict.

In those years when drinking restrictions were not being rigorously enforced, the Alberta had a long-standing policy of serving drinks on the house between the hours of six and nine in the morning, a sort of "hair of the dog" tradition said to be much appreciated by Bob Edwards.

In 1902 Perley sold the Alberta Hotel to Norman D. Jackson for a reported seventy thousand dollars. Then, in 1908, the Alberta passed into the hands of G. Kilbourn, who leased it to Charles D. Taprell.

Taprell was its last proprietor, for on 21 July 1916, liquor prohibition become law, thereby eliminating the hotel's main source of revenue and the venue for the town's finest discussions, idea sessions, arguments, and settlement of civic problems. In May 1916, R.B. Bennett was at his table for the final meal served by the Alberta Hotel.

The imaginative table d'hôte, the free morning drinks, the good conversational company of leading Calgarians, and the well-maintained rooms had made the Alberta Hotel a favourite Calgary stopping place for twenty-six busy years.

Fore!

IT IS SAID THAT CALGARY'S FIRST GOLF GAME took place in 1884 on a stretch of lumpy prairie grassland called Buffalo Wallow out near today's Mission district.

Calgary's first formal golf course was centred upon today's Fourth Street and Seventeenth Avenue SW intersection. In 1898 a group of townspeople bought six city lots for fifteen dollars each, and had registered the name, Calgary Golf Club. By 1899, the club had thirty-three members of which fifteen were women.

Then, as the town of Calgary continued to spread southward, the prairie golf course was shifted to today's Elbow Park area, near Elboya Bridge. The modest little wooden golf house stood near the modern intersection of Elbow Drive and Sifton Boulevard.

By 1903 the CPR sold some of its hillside and river-bottom acreage on the east side of the river to the renamed Calgary Golf and Country Club. The group president was David Jackson Young. An avid golfer, he had arrived from his native Nottingham, England, by way of Regina in 1893.

Another of Calgary's early golfing enthusiasts was John Hextall, the man responsible for the city's acquisition of Bowness Park. Hextall built a baronial Elizabethan-style clubhouse on a promontory of land overlooking Bowness and the park as well as his own half-timbered mansion west of the park entrance. It had generous overnight accommodation, being so far out of the city, and was a favourite dull-dress party rendezvous for young Calgarians.

St. Andrew's Golf Club, formed in April 1912, occupied some of the bald prairie hillside above West Hillhurst and Parkdale long before the city spread that far. The treeless, sun-drenched prairie grass course has long since vanished beneath the suburb of St. Andrew's Heights and the Foothills Hospital.

As kids, we used to loll in the cool shade of the big trees on the steep slope of Spruce Cliff and watch tiny figures plodding along at the St. Andrew's course. Somehow it never occurred to us to have anything to do with the golf courses, although we'd have developed an avid interest had we been told club-toting youths called "caddies" were actually paid to lug clubs for those sweaty players. From where we sat in the delicious and fragrant shade, the game they called "golf" looked like a heat-blistered drag.

We did develop a limited interest in the game, however, when we discovered how many club-swinging addicts lost their golf balls while playing the municipally owned Shaganappi Golf Course that parallelled the Banff Coach Road near Charlie Jackson's farm. We began to spend time diligently searching the grass along the Banff road. A ball in good shape would fetch as much as five cents. You gauged its secondhand worth to a golfer by the freshness of the enamelled dots and the condition of the word "Spalding" on the cover.

As for my involvement with the game itself, the story began in 1935 when I was a radio announcer with CJOR in Vancouver. One day I spotted a beautiful leather-trimmed golf bag, out of which poked a small nest of golf clubs. Despite my cruelly skimpy salary I felt I had to have the outfit.

The proprietor and I struck a deal. This traveller's "orphan" sample became mine for sixteen dollars—the sturdy, handsome bag with its beautiful chestnut brown leather handle, base, carrying strap, and trim, and the six matched steel-shafted clubs. These, I was assured, would perform wonderfully, last a long time, and, best of all, allow me to enhance my golf skills. Part of the sales pitch prediction turned out to be very true.

While I was at the Pacific coast, one of the radio station's engineers and I played twice. The Jericho golf course was laid out on a partially forested slope close to the ocean shore. One of the fairways had an uphill dog's leg to the right—exactly my style. Basil Hilton, my opponent and companion, kept saying stupid things like, "Don't forget to address the ball!" ("Hello, ball!") and "What's your handicap?," as though I had the faintest idea.

Anyway, this Jericho fairway—a broad, lush,

Golfer A. Carson McWilliams driving from hole number eleven, Calgary Municipal Golf Course, ca. 1920s. *Courtesy Glenbow-Alberta Institute/NA-1604-29*

green upslope—was curved to the right around a noble stand of tall old evergreens. By the time we reached the tee, Basil's score card read something like twelve while mine stood at around thirty-eight. In order to help me prune the total, he again showed me how to hold the club and (silently) address the teed-up ball.

I clenched my teeth, closed my eyes, and swung with all my might. For the first time I connected perfectly with the ball. I opened my eyes, in response to Basil's awed comment, to see the ball whiz up the hill, rise with a sense of majesty, clear the tree-tops, and swoop to the right out of sight. When we made our way around the hill we found that my golf ball lay about three feet from the flag and the cup. I had made the Par Three hole in two!

I could hardly wait for my next game at Jericho, this time accompanied by three fellows from the radio station. To everyone's amazement I again played that hole in two, which did a lot towards smoothing out my total score.

I played one more big-time game in 1950 at the end of the war. I had returned to the CBC from six years overseas and found myself and my half-dozen clubs as one of a foursome at the prestigious Royal Montreal Golf Club. The passing years had not helped my game. I recall trying to get off the first tee while the ball mocked me from the ground near my feet. Behind me other foursomes fretted at the hold-up as I continued to add points to my score before I even got off the first tee.

My next problem arose from the fact that in some places the fairways lie parallel to one another, and the golfers move along them in reverse directions. Twice, after having explored the woodlands in an unsuccessful attempt to find my golf ball, I emerged to stand out on the fairway with another ball "at the ready." But I was quickly admonished by other golfers for heading in the wrong direction.

Another fairway ducked under the railway where CN/CP Pool Trains raced between Montreal and Toronto. I did a "Jericho." I watched with horror as my high-flying curved ball blasted a window of a passenger coach as a train sped across a viaduct over the fairway. I hoped passengers were used to that hazard. My three companions were having their second drinks at the Nineteenth by the time I chipped and replaced divots up to the clubhouse between stepping aside to let other golfers play through.

I never did play again because my dearest high school friend spotted my almost new clubs and handsome bag when I returned to Calgary in the early 1950s. He gladly paid me twenty-six dollars for the set and told me a while ago that those same half-dozen matched steel-shafted clubs continue to be the mainstay of his game. That strikes me as quite a record for a set of fifty-six-year-old golfing sticks and bag.

I notice that wherever you look today, from Country Hills NW to Crystalaire in Okotoks, it appears mandatory for every clutch of new homes to have an eighteen-hole golf course. It seems developers are very confident of attracting their share of divot-digging duffers. Let's hope, if they golf as well I do, that someone has taken the precaution of warning passing motorists!

The Nodwell Giants

*O*NE COULD NEVER CALL W. BRUCE NODWELL a stick-in-the-mud. Bruce and his brothers, Jack and Roy, were born on a farm near Asquith, west of Saskatoon. Their farm was close to the CNR tracks along which the Silk Trains would occasionally hurtle on their way to New York. When the Canadian National lost the high-speed contract things grew rather dull for the active youngsters, so they dreamed up a scheme to "capture" some people to talk to, perhaps even play with.

The boys hauled buckets of water over to a low spot in the dirt road at the front of the place and created their own mudhole. Fortunately for their "victims," the boys were unsuccessful in bogging down the few cars that passed, even with the added attraction of a few tacks on the road. Little did young Bruce Nodwell know that his mudpuddle idea would parlay itself into a lifetime of accomplishment.

During the Depression, Bruce took any job he could find, from setting pins in a bowling alley to driving trucks. He and Phyllis, his Banff-born wife, lived in nearly a dozen places in western Canada. But ultimately Bruce Nodwell and the oil patch got together after he and Phyllis made their home in Calgary while he worked at the B.A. Oil Refinery, then with Texaco.

The mud was about to re-enter Bruce's life. Petroleum exploration was an awakening giant. Alberta-based companies started to probe all over the province, especially in wilderness areas. They urgently required transportation capable of tackling the most challenging terrain and were scouring the continent, as far afield as Moline and Pittsburgh, for big, tough vehicles. The Bombardier people of Quebec were already building a tracked vehicle, offspring of their own invention, the snowmobile, but it could carry only three thousand pounds of payload. Imperial Oil of Calgary, in the vanguard of far-flung exploration needed a freight carrier capable of a five-ton load while still treading lightly on the soggy northern muskeg. They hired a Texan to design such a vehicle.

The Nodwells, whose factory was in the Manchester industrial area of Calgary, transformed blueprints into reality. It was a grotesque vehicle designed to exert only two pounds per square inch on anything it crawled across. Before it even rumbled out of the shop the Texan engineer fled saying, as he went, that he was scared of it and didn't think it would work. At that time he was right. But Imperial Oil and Bruce persisted, incorporating their own ideas and those of Bill Coulson, an old family friend and expert machinist. Not long after the Leduc oil discovery the "North King," their giant creation, rolled out of their southeast Calgary shop, proof positive that "Calgary could do it!"

The Nodwell's crack salesman, Ted Riback, soon had orders for fourteen North Kings, a dozen of them destined for wilderness petroleum explo-

The Nodwell Tracked Carrier and other such vehicles, designed and built in Calgary, have found a ready market all over the world. *Courtesy Glenbow-Alberta Institute/NA-2408-26*

ration, the other two for the Canadian army and air force.

Robin-Nodwell Manufacturing Limited was on a roll. Powered by two GM diesel engines each, six machines were shipped by rail and sea from Calgary to the hitherto impassable hinterland of eastern Venezuela. A sales representative from Bogota flew to Calgary to spend two weeks studying the construction and performance of the Nodwell machines. Observers of prospective customers began converging on the Manchester site. Bruce gave them some action-packed proof. A giant mudhole version of Bruce's childhood years appeared on the plant's acreage. Roaring and sloshing through the deep bog he had created, his huge wilderness carriers proved their worth, such a contrast to the Asquith road days when the skimpy-powered Fords, Stars, and Chevs had slithered through the boys' most valiant barriers–with or without added tacks.

Nodwell's progeny were impressive for those days. Two of the models produced had a gross laden weight of 53,000 and 27,200 pounds yet had a ground-bearing pressure of only two pounds per square inch. A woman of average build wearing high-heeled shoes would bring down all her weight on an area of less than a square inch. For all her walking heft she would have been dwarfed by the Model R's 34,000-pound weight, its 29,000-square-inch of load area measuring eight by twenty feet, its stance of eight feet four inches from ground to cab roof, and its ability to also carry an 18,000-pound winch while travelling up to ten miles per hour!

With only a limited market for such big machines the Nodwell enterprise, in 1954, was compelled to diversify its output. It earned a good reputation as a producer of storage tanks, bridge rails, and other heavy metal construction components for which there was a ready, though highly competitive, market. Meanwhile Bruce and the firm's designers burned midnight oil at their drawing boards in preparation for one more assault upon the wilderness vehicle venture until one day the Nodwell Scout Carrier rolled out of the shop. In essence it was an open platform for a 2,100-pound machinery load, or for a closed personnel-carrying cabin. It was capable of a speed of twenty-five mph on its broad tracks while treading almost delicately at less than two pounds to the square inch on unstable wet ground, far less than a tractor, truck, automobile, or even human foot.

Acceptance was immediate, and the Scout became a universal crosscountry transporter for petroleum, power, lumber, and telephone companies. The Nodwell name soon became synonymous with motorized wilderness penetration of all types of terrain including acres of ancient swampland. More than that, the Nodwell assembly line diversified by turning out eight powerful tracked, airport fire-rescue trucks for the government of India.

Shortly before handing over the reins of the firm to his son Jack, Bruce Nodwell told me of a memorable field test. Chevron Oil of California had invited rival firms to bring their prized vehicles to Alaska for a sub-Arctic equipment tryout. Nodwell's ace driver Jack Smith and his machine turned in an outstanding performance that resulted in the Calgary firm being chosen as the supplier of all the oil explorer's wilderness vehicles. It was a historic international recognition of the quality of Calgary designed, made, and built equipment.

Next was a visit by Soviet Union oilmen for a winter demonstration including work in the Nodwell's testing ground giant "mud puddle." It happened that the head of the delegation was the country's minister of petroleum, who, in his younger years, had been a heavy equipment driver. Through an interpreter he made it known that he would test drive the Nodwell machines, which he intended to put through the most punishing of all paces. The result was his country's order for an initial thirty-three machines and the comment, "This is what we have been looking for."

Today, under the very suitable name of Foremost International Industries, Inc., president Jack Nodwell guides his manufacturing, designing, and sales teams at the plant anchoring the northeast corner of our foothills city. An impressive parade of ungainly vehicles capable of accomplishing almost impossible transportation tasks is constantly outbound from Calgary to the far corners of the globe.

Bruce Nodwell is retired now, dividing his time between the forested tranquillity of British Columbia and the bright warmth of southern California. He has two indelible memories from among a host of reminiscences of his productive life. When the Soviet Union oil minister climbed down from one of the giant vehicles he had just finished testing, he pinned a badge on Bruce naming him an honorary member of Engineers of the USSR. And in 1971, facing Roland Michener, governor general of Canada, Bruce, once the mud-puddler of Asquith, was invested with the Order of Canada in worthy recognition of his contribution to opening up our nation's north.

Two-wheeled Terror

THERE WAS A TIME WHEN RIDING A BICYCLE IN Calgary was less crowded than it is today. Some say it was safer back then, but I'm not so sure . . .

"Never ride as a passenger on the bar of a bike!" I was cautioned. But when Teddy Britton offered me a lift to Western Canada High one afternoon, it was too good an invitation to resist. So I hopped aboard, sidesaddle as it were, on the bar of his brand new department store bike and away we went, east along Prospect Avenue, then swooping down Hope Street.

Down indeed! A city water department crew had not quite finished a trench stretching across the street, so there was a slash a couple of inches below the pavement's surface. We hit it at a good speed and the bicycle's front forks buckled like milk shake straws. I flew one way, and Teddy another. I still have the scars on the inside of my elbows. I also skinned my forehead from that swan dive to the pavement, but it grew back without a mark. I left a good part of my hide on that piece of Hope Street's hill.

A couple of years before that episode, I had blown all my savings on a CCM Bluebird drop-bar, twenty-twenty-two-inch beauty with a padded leather Parson's coil-spring saddle, box handlebars, Hercules coaster brake, and drop-sided mudguards. One busy afternoon in light drizzle I was standing on the pedals, pumping across the Fourth Street West level crossing. The subway wasn't built back then and the train tracks were slippery. Suddenly, WHAP!, the back wheel skidded and I and my beautiful blue bike slid under the shaggy hooves of a Percheron pulling a moving van. In the instant I lay on the pavement this huge hoof seemed to blot out the daylight. It hesitated inches from my face, then gently settled next to my head, making spaghetti of the rim and spokes of the bike's back wheel.

I was hauled out from under, weeping with fright, but immeasurably grateful for the thoughtfulness of the huge horse. I could not afford a new steel-rimmed wheel, and the Bluebird was probably the only one in town with a steel front wheel and a wooden rimmed rear one.

In recent times I spent a couple of painful hours aboard what today is called a bicycle. I had trouble with the handlebars. In Bluebird days, the box handlebars swooped back and up to where your hands naturally were. They had a cross-bar to stabilize a parcel or, better yet, as an alternative hand-hold. This "modern" ten-speed bike had ram's horns curving down and back so that your butt was up in the air and your hands and head down among a gaggle of brake levers and long aimless cables.

In this ape-posture you have to crick your neck upwards to see where you are going, while your elevated rear end is perched on a little unyielding leather doily I was told is a seat. I wondered what

CPR telegraph messengers in the days when things moved at a more leisurely pace, April 1924. Note the box handlebars on the bicycles. *Courtesy Glenbow-Alberta Institute/ND-3-2322*

had been so wrong about sitting upright to see where you were going, with the weather-proof coaster brake ready to grip at the slightest back-pedal. And this thing has no mudguards, so any bit of road dampness spatters you, adding to the discomfort of your hunched back, scrunched innards, and warped eyeballs.

I have been told this is a racing bike design, a concept that, to me, is as practical as driving a supercharged turbo Indy car in a thirty-kilometre speed zone. Oh yes, this contraption admittedly is a featherweight, so much lighter than the Bluebird that was designed for comfortable upright cruising. Today's wheels have an assortment of gears to rival those of a Peterbilt eighteen-wheeler. But all of this exposed-to-the-weather derailer, or relayer, whatever, has me wondering what fate had befallen the reliable fully enclosed Sturmy-Archer brake and gearbox combination that operated so unobtrusively between handlebars and the rear hub. Mind you, even one of today's gut-crunching velodrome jobs is an improvement over the bike on which I learned to ride.

When I was growing up, all the roads in Killarney and Glengarry were dirt except for the improved main ones, which were coated with loose gravel. One day Father brought home a woman's very old white bike, liberated from a city truck heading for the incinerator at Fourteenth Street and Ninth Avenue West.

In a few days he had it running with the addition of a secondhand seat, chain, and one tire from Iddiols Brothers' locksmith and bicycle shop next to City Hall. There were two major problems with that bike. It must have been built for a giraffe of a woman. Mercifully, for me, it had no crossbar. It had fixed drive, which meant either you pedalled constantly, or held your feet safely away from the churning pedals while you coasted.

My sister, Mary, nearly three years my senior, was custodian of this infernal machine. Fortunately, she found it tiresome to ride, so I sort of inherited it. Because I was anything but tall I had to stand on the pedals, pumping them until I got up speed, steering with the handlebars at eye-level. Then, when it was time to coast, I learned to hop backwards and upwards onto the saddle, landing there with my feet akimbo. At the point of stalling I had to aim my feet at the whirling pedals without bringing the bike and me to a tangled and often gravelly halt.

I became so adept at this I once tried showing off with a "look, no hands" stance up on my high perch. I passed two clearly impressed girls in splendid fashion, but in a moment, the stony road took its toll. Those scars were added to my collection.

In high school days we often rode our bicycles across Glengarry to South Calgary High. It was open prairie back then, with single-rutted cowpath trails across the slightly rolling emptiness. After school, on occasion, instead of taking a shortcut, it was necessary to ride down Fourteenth Street, pick up a parcel for someone in the family, then toil westward up the Seventeenth Avenue hill.

Thereby hangs a painful and almost devastating tale. I admit that riding one of those heavy single-speed bicycles had it drawbacks. The sensible procedure was to walk up steeper slopes, probably accounting for the fact that the British used the term "push-bike." On this occasion, to avoid toiling upward on foot with the bike as well as the parcel, it seemed mildly logical to pedal as far as I could.

That is what I was doing, only just making headway by standing on the pedals, when the chain broke! It was sudden; it was excruciating. I writhed at the roadside convinced that henceforth I would be singing soprano in the church choir.

I know bicycle riding is renowned as a health-promoting pastime. I should know because I became much healthier when I quit.

Curing the "Sick Kids"

CALGARY WAS THE FIRST CENTRE IN CANADA to create a Junior Red Cross Hospital. I recall being recruited as a member of the organization's junior branch in my earliest public school years. In order to be "one of the crowd" we not only wore a red-and-white celluloid pin-on Red Cross badge, we openly bragged about our affiliation.

Forty-one-thousand students donated a portion of our tiny weekly allowance as our contribution to "curing the sick kids." Our collective donations took care of a large portion of the expenses of running the thirty-five-bed hospital located (and still standing) at 522 Eighteenth Avenue SW. Calgary's Junior Red Cross Society was a brave one, for the pioneering venture was launched with financial assets of about $669, plus a great deal of faith and selfless volunteer dedication by individuals and families throughout the city.

It was in May 1922 when the Junior Red Cross Crippled Children's Hospital opened its doors to patients from all over the province. The official opening was performed by Dr. Robert George Brett, Alberta's lieutenant governor and honorary president of our province's branch of the Red Cross Society. The building had been a family mansion, but a very determined group of children's Hospital Aid and local Kinsmen's club workers soon whipped it into shape under the eagle-eyed leadership of matron L.B. Peat. At the end of hostilities in Europe, the hospital came into its own. It did its best, with the very limited knowledge of the time, to tend to some young victims of the 1919 influenza epidemic cruelly sweeping the world.

Around this time I was a spoiled, over-indulged brat aged about six. One day, the young 'flu convalescents were being treated to an exciting and very special country outing–a carefully planned sports day. On crutches, in wheel chairs, and in nurses' and doctors' arms they had been taken out to the western edge of the city to the old E.H. Crandell home at Brickburn (now known as the Stu Hart residence below Broadcast Hill). For some events, such as foot races, we–a handful of healthy young invitees–were allowed to compete.

During one of the races on a specially constructed cinder track I tripped over my own two left feet and skinned both knees. My initial bellowing by far exceeded my "injuries," which were promptly treated with iodine and bandages by one of the nurses. Included in her first aid treatment was a sharply worded lecture for my cry-baby performance in front of the truly sick children.

Following in, and obviously more than adequately filling, the admirable footsteps of founding matron Peat, was matron nurse Florence Reid, who arrived here in 1928 and became the Director of Nursing for the Canadian Red Cross Society. There was a dire need for better and larger facilities. So the Junior Red Cross Hospital moved a few blocks southwest to lower Mount Royal to take over the old Vital Raby mansion, once the home of a pioneer wine merchant's family. When R.B. Bennett acquired the property the house was vacant, and he donated it to the Red Cross with the aim of concentrating on the orthopaedic requirements of the youngsters.

It was a spacious three-storey red brick mansion at 1009 Twentieth (Royal) Avenue SW. Two floors had sweeping verandahs, which, when glassed in, became splendid sun-drenched recuperative wards for the children. School classes were introduced during the two decades the hospital was located there, and in the 1930s Eileen Nicholson and I—members of the Tenth Boy Scout Troop—ran a Wolf Cub Pack there. It was a humbling challenge for us to devise methods of instructing our very young charges in woodcraft, hobbies, and outdoor camping and nature lore when every one of them was bedridden.

The setting was most incongruous despite the eager enthusiasm of the otherwise bored youngsters, for we taught them semaphore signalling, citizenship responsibilities, wilderness survival, plant and wildlife recognition, in an atmosphere laden with turn-of-the-century opulence and decor composed of rich panelling, ornate lighting, and gleaming oaken trim and flooring, all of which was inherited, as it were, from the Raby's wealthy lifestyle.

The hospital's orthopaedic surgeon was McGill-University-trained Dr. Reginald Deane, the son of mounted police superintendent Richard Burton Deane. For fourteen years, from 1922 to 1936, Dr. Deane provided voluntary orthopaedic services. In 1931 the dedicated doctor voiced his concern for the safety of the little patients in eight cots located in the attic of the house should ever there be a fire. That concern elicited a response that was typical of the extent of voluntary community involvement in the venture. Members of the Calgary Fire Department, under the guidance of chief James "Cappy" Smart, built chute slides from those upper windows for emergency evacuation of the bed-ridden children, a precaution that, fortunately, was never needed.

Little was known, in those days, of certain ailments that bedeviled the young patients, many of whom were hospitalized far from home and family. Treatment was long, detailed, and, in some cases, purely experimental. From all over the province came victims of ailments such as tuberculosis, osteomyelitis, cleft palates, club feet, misshapen spines, and infantile paralysis. The latter cruelly stalked young people many years later, particularly in the 1930s, when it struck in a most haphazard, vicious, and unpredictable pattern.

Those were the days of the Great Depression when salaries for well-qualified help reached a discouragingly low ebb. The senior graduate nurse, in addition to her board and room, was paid eight dollars per month. Three senior nurses each received forty dollars, the pair of juniors were paid twenty-five dollars monthly, and the third junior had a choice: either leave the hospital or agree to be paid fifteen dollars a month while, as a term of her employment, also performing the duties of a kitchen maid. She chose to stay.

Because of the lengthy treatment of some of the young patients, it was necessary to set up school classes. Mrs. Mabel Mappin began teaching in the hospital in 1932, using Alberta's departmental curriculum. She and her successors taught grades one to twelve. Departmental examinations were held even though many of the pupils were completely bed-ridden. A hospital school library was

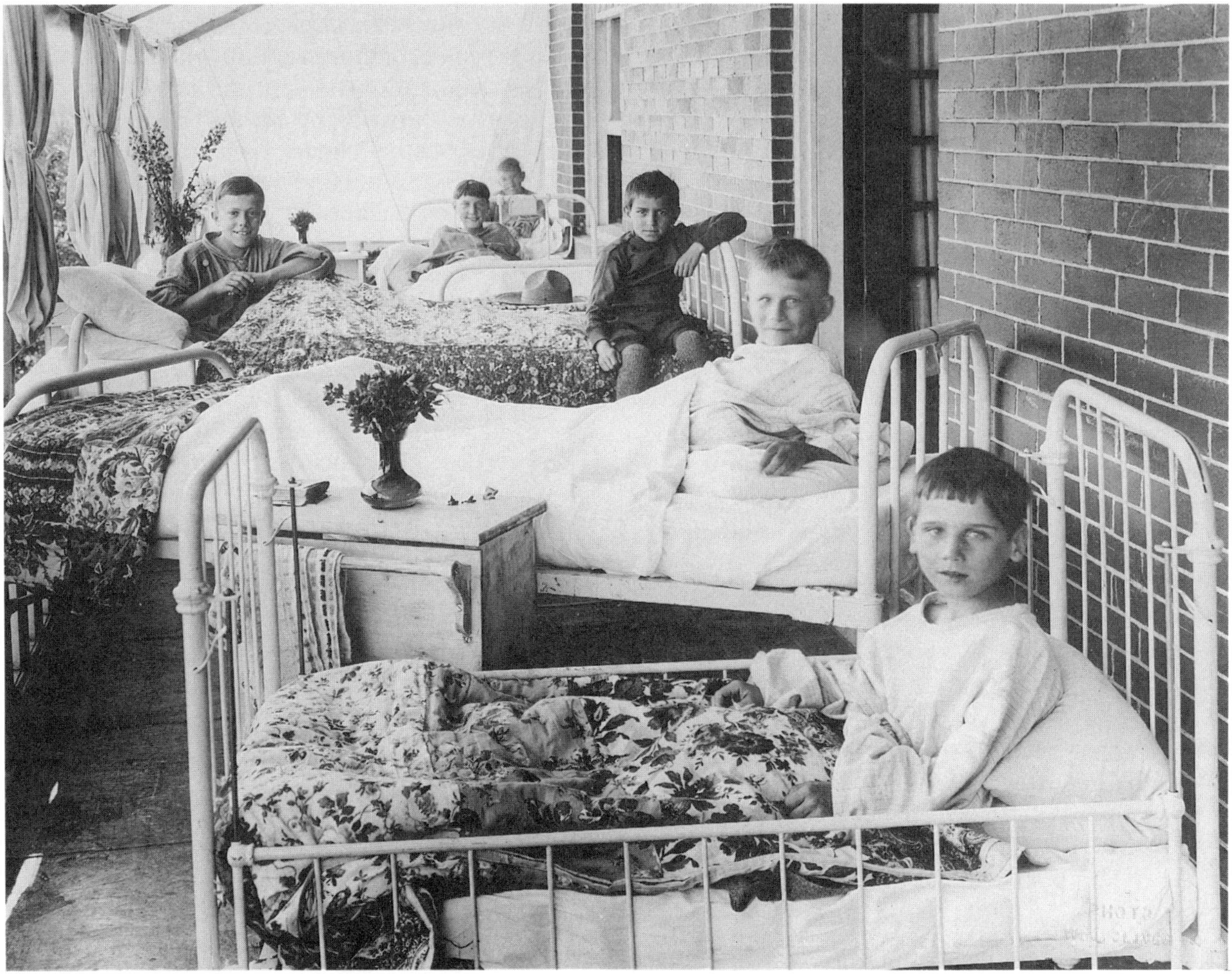

Young patients on the verandah of the Junior Red Cross Hospital, 1922. *Courtesy Glenbow-Alberta Institute/NA-2903-1*

formed and continued to grow, thanks to public donations. Handicrafts were also a part of the program at the hospital, to strength and rehabilitate wasted motor functions. One of the long-term volunteers, Walter Ricks, held basket-making classes every week. The special skills and interests of James Mather and his namesake son resulted in the manufacture of in-house prosthetics, augmented by the skills of Mildred Spreckley, Calgary's first trained physiotherapist.

Another therapeutic procedure involved singing and speech instruction. For the strengthening of the spirit (although the morale and courage of the stoical little people was of legendary calibre), a roster of visiting chaplains undertook religious instruction. World War II brought with it an unfortunate delay in the expansion of the hospital. However, in 1946, when the city donated land, plans were completed for a long overdue and much-needed new children's hospital. The new Richmond Road 150-bed facility was opened on 3 March 1951. Among those who rejoiced at the ceremony was Florence E.C. Reid. Having been named field organizer and nursing supervisor of the Alberta Division of the Canadian Red Cross Society in 1932, Miss Reid had been appointed the hospital's matron in 1933. She was an honoured recipient of the King George V Jubilee medal in 1935 and was recognized by the Chamber of Commerce as an outstanding citizen of Calgary in 1953.

In recent years at least a dozen new services, including the in-patient care of emotionally disturbed youngsters, have been added to what, since November 1959, has been called the Alberta Children's Hospital. It is a large and complex operation in these modern times. Its scope, skills, and accomplishments are worthy of much admiration. It is a fine legacy to the community spirit that started it all: children carefully hoarding their pennies and nickels to lend a hand to the those stricken by illness.

The Art of Signing

WHEN SETTLERS CONGREGATED IN THE SETTLEment of Calgary it was logical that they use the walls and facades of their business premises to announce their skills and wares to fellow townspeople. Hence even the more modestly proportioned buildings of low profile became nearly saturated with signs.

In 1900, English immigrant George Lawton Taylor brought a new dimension to Calgary outdoor advertising by opening a professional sign painting business on the second floor of the Co-op Block at 221B Eighth Avenue East. His quality output rapidly replaced the rough hand-painted signs and written handbills seen and distributed in the little settlement since its establishment. The new company flourished, and throughout today's downtown Calgary one still encounters a few weathered relics of Taylor's wall signs painted on brick, metal, concrete, and sandstone. He was not without competition back then, from the growing number of rival sign firms such as Globe, Art, Snowdon, A-1, Calgary Bill Posting, Hook, and others. All but two have vanished with the passing years.

Obviously there was no shortage of customers, for the sign painters had to brave the pranks and fickleness of Calgary weather, using ropes, planks, and grapples that would seem primitive by today's standards. Clearly Calgary's administrators had no interest in governing the quality and quantity of outdoor business signs. At an early stage in its lifetime the city of Lethbridge legislated against business signs that would have overhung the sidewalks. Downtown pedestrians were to have an unimpeded view of the clear Alberta sky. On the other hand, Calgary has had an ongoing job of tidying and restricting the use of outdoor signage. Despite setting standards from time to time we continue to suffer from a clutter of such business advertising.

In the first decade of this century Calgary's midtown building walls bore many giant advertisements:

THE H.A. HICKS INVESTMENT COMPANY

BINDERS, MOWERS, DRILLS, RAKES, PLOWS, WAGONS,
HARROWS—THE MASSEY-HARRIS CO. LIMITED

CUSHING BROS. CO. LIMITED

A sign almost as large as the single-storey premises on which it was painted advertised:

CITY PROPERTY, FARM LANDS,
GRAHAM, HAMILTON, CAMPBELL LIMITED,
LOANS, INSURANCE, RENTALS

KING GEORGE HOTEL—EUROPEAN PLAN—FIREPROOF—
HOT AND COLD RUNNING WATER IN EVERY ROOM

and, of course, hundreds more wherever one's glance happened to fall upon a storefront or a tall or stubby building wall. They advertised the premises of wholesale provisioners, restaurants, piano stores, furniture emporiums, and drugstores. Many spaces, of course, had nothing to do with the business on location but were rented to other firms who wanted to keep their name constantly before the public. All merchants hoped pedestrians might glance heavenward while walking along well-travelled streets and avenues.

One memorable sign was of a huge griffin, the symbol of Parker Brothers department store on the north side of Seventh Avenue at First Street West opposite the Hudson's Bay Company. That big beast, which occupied the upper

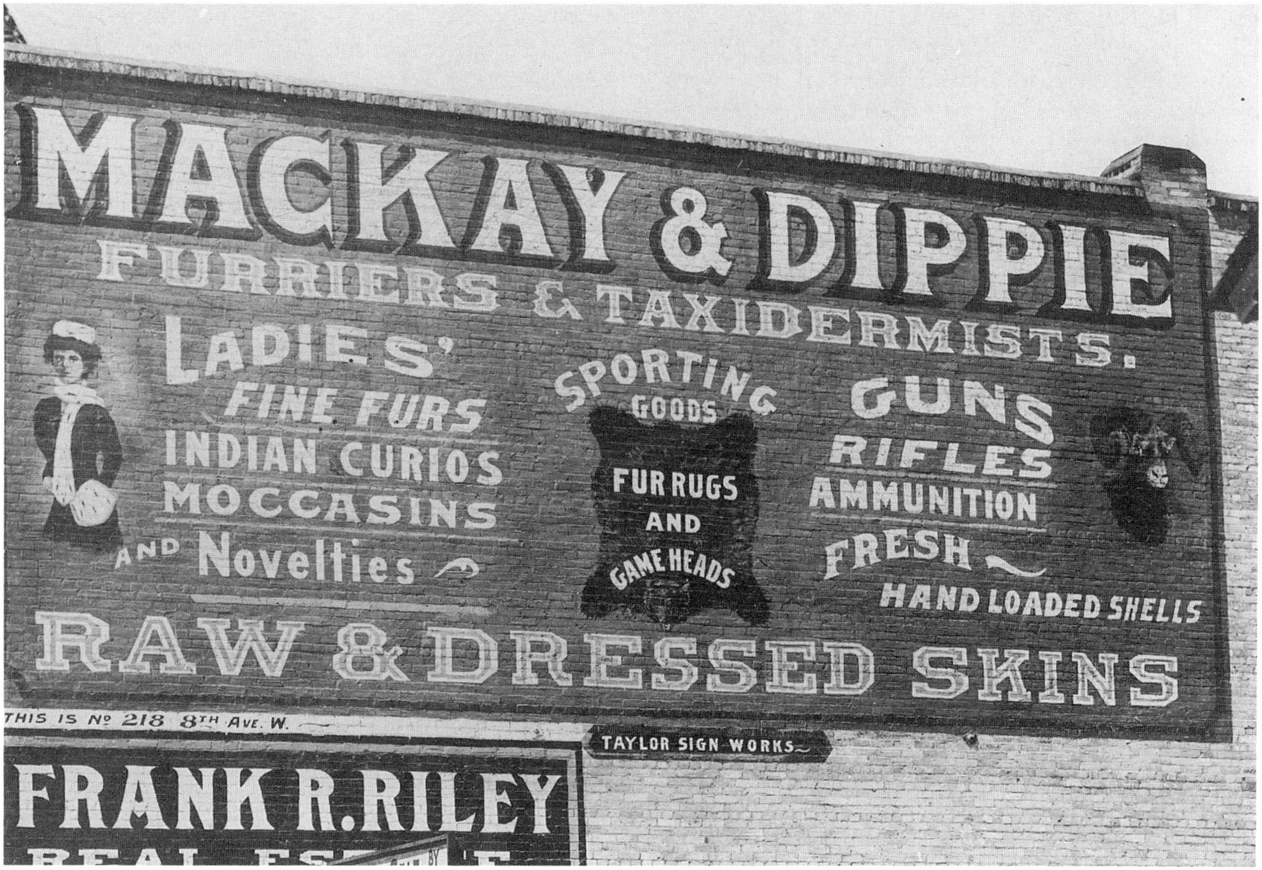

A typical example of the signs that "graced" city buildings in the 1930s and 1940s when the skyline of Calgary was "lowrise" and such ads could be seen easily by pedestrians. *Courtesy Glenbow-Alberta Institute/NA-3795-12*

part of the building's west wall, was replaced, in time, by THE HERALD GOES HOME, the slogan of the newspaper at the time it moved into the Southam Building, took over the site of the defunct department store, and renamed the structure the Herald Building.

One odd sign punctuated a staircase in the Clarence Block on Eighth Avenue a few doors east of the Bank of Montreal. It led up to Robinson's Clothing store, which, because it was not at street level, enjoyed a lower rent. Hence it was able to paint each riser so that a potential economy-minded customer could be urged to WALK UPSTAIRS AND SAVE TEN.

Then, of course, there were the billboards themselves, which, as a rough estimate, sprang up on half the vacant lots around the centre of town and its immediate surroundings. For example, before the T. Eaton Company built its department store between Third and Fourth streets, and Eighth and Seventh avenues West, that city block was almost completely edged with billboards. Behind them, in the shelter from hot summer sun and cold winter winds, Sarcee Indians parked their buggies and horse teams while they went about their shopping.

It was Ogden Nash who, many years ago, spoke for many like-minded city and country people by deploring the excessive and aggressive use of billboards. His rueful Joyce Kilmeresque quatrain was:

I think that I shall never see
A billboard lovely as a tree–
In fact, unless the billboards fall
I'll never see a tree at all.

One of Calgary's truly memorable billboards faced us from the crest of Tom Campbell's Hill, and in fact, was the reason for its name. Local hatter Tom Campbell made Smile Hats and his symbol was a Kewpie Doll, naked except for a Smile top hat and a walking stick very strategically placed to preserve the decency of the nude little pot-bellied male elf. The very large sign was famous for its daring, its location, and its visibility, declaring to all Calgarians, "The Naked Truth is Not Immodest."

An outdoor sign of the 1920s and 1930s decorated the east wall of Mackay and Dippie's premises on Eighth Avenue West between First and Second streets. It advertised Ladies' Fine Furs, Indian Curios, Moccasins, Guns, Rifles, Ammunition, and Raw and Dressed Skins. It lent a very authentic western flavour to our midtown business district.

Probably the fanciest wall sign in yesterday's Calgary decorated a wall of the West End Heating Company. It featured a Front Rank Hot Air Furnace. Around it pranced small, harassed red devils with arrow tails. They were uttering complaints regarding the extraordinary efficiency of the furnace: "Good-bye, We're Going Home!" and "It's Too Hot for Us Here."

A record-breaking Calgary sign was said to be the longest in western Canada. It stretched for ninety-four metres–high up along a towering street-side flour mill wall in Bonnybrook. There, for all to see, be they teamsters, motorists, pedestrians, or street car riders, were the huge proud words SPILLERS CANADIAN MILLING COMPANY LIMITED. That was the longest one-liner in Calgary.

One "billboard adventure" in particular has left an indelible impression upon me. I was about thirteen years old and very unworldly. My mother must have persuaded my father that the time had come to have "that conversation with the boy." It seemed to be a rather aimless pursuit but I was persuaded to walk with Father from our Twenty-eighth Street West home in Glengarry down to the foot of the Seventeenth Avenue hill on some trivial errand, then wander back up the hill home again.

I recall reaching the intersection of Seventeenth Avenue and Fourteenth Street West where, just beyond the southeast corner was a large lone billboard. I didn't realize it but bill-posters had just reached the permissive plateau that allowed the advertising of "intimate women's things." This particular sign-board was an over-all chaste dark blue with, two words in large pristine white letters: MODESS BECAUSE . . .

So well I remember Father shyly drawing my attention to the billboard and asking, "You know what that means?" A mysterious intuition whispered to me in my innocence, so I airily replied, "Oh sure!" even though I hadn't a clue. Father sighed with relief as we set off back up the hill—and that was the full extent of our only father-son talk about birds and bees. Some time later, when I really learned what the sign meant, I wondered how well my father had fibbed to Mother about that encounter with a billboard.

Heaven on Ice

AT THIS ALTITUDE AND LATITUDE, WHERE WE normally have chilly weather most of the year, it is not surprising that so many Calgarians are accomplished skaters. Of course, we dote on those who, as team members in numbered jerseys, helmets, and face guards, hurtle about the ice in pursuit of a puck; and we gasp with admiration at those who perform near miracles of balance and grace in the realm of figure skating.

It seems to me that this part of Canada has produced a formidable corps of experts on blades who have caused the legendary Hans Brinker and His Silver Skates of our childhood folklore to blush at his inadequacy. Come to think of it, we had a newcomer kid on our block in Killarney who arrived from his native Holland with skates just like those in the pictures of Hans Brinker. They were bulbous, shoe-length, and made of smoothly finished hardwood. A slit along the base revealed a steel skate blade. We all wanted to try them, never having seen anything of the kind, but despite their portability, he was probably very wise to refuse us. They fastened to the soles of his shoes by adjustable, clutching metal frames that he tightened with a key. They attached in the same way rollerskates were temporarily affixed to sturdy boots.

Do you remember your first excursion on the "silver blades"? Mine was on the winter-flooded potato patch in our back yard. The skate blades, made by CCM, the Canada Cycle and Motor Company, had been a Christmas present. Next came a parental selection of the sturdy, well-used, ankle-high laced boots. Father took blades and boots to his workshop in the basement and, after figuring the left from the right, returned with the blades screwed to the soles. Because the little screws had to be fat, yet short, the boots were worn with the addition of a protective felt insole so that the tips of the screws would not pierce tender junior-sized feet.

I was not used to wearing two pairs of socks in those boots and it made them very tight. But it was necessary to ward off the cold. Father had banked the edges of the potato patch and flooded it into a passable sheet of ice. Then, swathed in far too many scarfs, mitts, sweaters, toque, and coat, I was turned loose, looking like Tweedledum or his twin brother. I spent most of my time like a run-down spinning top, skates in the air, nuzzling the ice.

In time I was allowed to use an old wooden kitchen chair that served as a novice skater's equivalent to an "old folks'" walker. While it saved me from many undignified tumbles, after a while it was haughtily discarded, for I had proved I could "skate" on my inside ankle bones as clumsily as any kid on the block.

The next step was to one of those neighbourhood sheets of ice often twinned with a hockey rink, the surfaces of which were renewed throughout the winter by the fire department's hoses. It was all well and good to have smooth

Skaters enjoying themselves on the Elbow River. *Courtesy Glenbow-Alberta Institute/NA-4910-4*

skating ice, but it didn't solve the problem of balancing on those blades. For a long time there was no money in the family's piggy-bank for a "boughten" skating-boot-and-blade outfit. Although one year I remember my sister Mary got an elegant secondhand pair of high-laced, shiny white figure-skating boots equipped with the longest blades I had ever seen. They had curled-up fronts cut with little spikes.

However, my turn came, and the Christmas arrival of a real set was all the more memorable. The boots and skates were rivetted together. The boots had a felt lining and built-in diagonal ankle support straps and buckles. The only uncooperative ingredients were my ankles, which wobbled and fell in abject obeisance to the law of gravitation, so my skate blades were always hazardously rounded. And that was despite Mr. Keen who, at his neighbourhood boot shop, guaranteed his skate-blade servicing to be "hollow ground." (For some time that expression baffled me, because it seemed better suited to things ecclesiastical. Father explained that hallowed ground was quite a different thing from Mr. Keen's grinder!)

A new kind of skate then appeared on the market and on the ice, of Calgary rinks—the tube skate. All but the blade itself was shaped like slim tubes. I, however, was far too preoccupied with policing my ankles and getting good use of my rivetted pair of blades. My next step was to feel competent enough to join the skaters under the lights at the big outdoor Hillhurst Rink on Sixth

Avenue NW. Another rink we reached by streetcar on a Saturday evening was the Arena, the vaulted wooden building at the fairgrounds close to the site of today's Corral. Certain times were set aside for pleasure skating only, and Ted Forsee and three or four other musicians sat in an open booth above the rink level giving us music to skate by. Monitors patrolled the ice to ensure all skaters were given a chance to dance, swoop, flail, or fall without fear of being harassed by speedsters, figure skaters, or hockey sticks.

There always was room, despite the crowds at the very popular place, for little kids who lived down Victoria Park way. They moved along hugging the boards, skating or hobbling on their ankles and blunted blades like little woolly wounded birds, occasionally windmilling their arms for balance. For those of us who had mastered the fundamentals and had reached our high school years, the Arena was a dreamy place to swoop around, cross-handed with one's favourite girl of that particular week.

One exciting thing we did on each of several winters was to skate in the moonlight on the Elbow River from Weasel Head to Elboya before there was a Glenmore Dam. With Mother, Father, and some of their friends with children, we drove to Weasel Head where we bundled up for the long serpentine trip down the river. The car drivers would return to town and have a small fire heating cocoa in the shadow of the old iron Elboya Bridge. Even during the coldest weather we had to beware of ominous black tongues of open water. Father, an excellent skater, led the way, steering us at our thunking speed down the succession of little frozen cascade bumps of the Elbow.

Community rinks of various sizes were scattered all over the little city, many with loudspeakers that played music for evening skating. Longtime Calgarian Phyllis Moore recently shared some skating memories with me from back in the days between about 1924 and 1930 when she used to frequent the community rink close to the site of the Calgary Tennis Club:

> There was free skating from nine to ten, no children allowed, so teenagers hustled to the rink drawn by the sound of "The Skaters' Waltz." It was not long before the single skaters became duos. Young men came and asked us formally, as if at a dance, for a skate, and you drifted away, lost in the sound of the music, the glamour of the partner, and the sheer pleasure of having left homework behind. It was the ultimate opportunity to hold your girl a bit close, to protect her, and to show her just what a fine fellow you were.
>
> The night went all too fast. The records for this era were "Little Spanish Town," "Constantinople," "Five Foot Two," "Louise," and at the end, "The Skaters' Waltz." The boys grasped wooden snow shovels and cleared the ice. It was part of a ritual; it helped the caretaker and put them in good standing with him. Then the caretaker dimmed the lights and it was time to go home. Pairs of young people walked slowly away, joining other pairs, gallant boys carrying two pairs of skates over their shoulders and keeping the young ladies' hands warm. These were the years when even a dime was hard to come by and the community rink was a godsend, with such warmth, such pleasure, and such identification with each other.

Sounds wonderful, doesn't it?

Bottoms Up

IN 1886 THE ONE THOUSAND OR SO RESIDENTS of the two-year-old town of Calgary added a new dimension to their social life by holding a Calgary Fair. That also was the year the first railway train completed its run from Montreal to the pacific coast, so local townsfolk had a perfect excuse to urge relatives "down east" to come and have a look at the fast-developing frontier.

The fair was a small but significant beginning to the staging, in 1908, of the Dominion Exhibition, which turned out to be a very popular family attraction. In those pre-refrigeration days it was not easy to display homegrown edibles, but farm wives, in particular, brought exhibition cooked foods and bottled preserves. Their menfolk groomed and showed their cherished livestock for judging at the family-oriented display and competition.

Urban gardeners brought their best vegetables and flowers to be adjudicated. Town and country school children proffered for the judges' opinions, their collection of carefully mounted leaves, flowers, insects, stamps, cigarette cards, medallions, buttons, and collectibles of all sorts for display and ribbons at the big fair.

Thus family involvement grew in step with the exhibition, which, by 1912, had developed into the Calgary Exhibition and Stampede. Thanks in great part to Canadian Pacific Railway's far-flung advertising for railway tourists, it was an event that attracted visitors from afar as well as nearby.

The extent of family participation was apparent in the calendar of attractions at the 1919 Calgary Stampede Peace Celebrations, following the Armistice ending World War I. Our leading retailer, the Hudson's Bay Company, bought facing pages in the Stampede souvenir program in order to: "Extend a Hearty Welcome to all Stampede Visitors." The message to visiting women declared:

> You are fortunate in being able to be present at the greatest Stampede ever held, and you are also fortunate in being able to inspect the newest fashions for Fall, 1919, surely one of the most important Fashion Expositions held for many years past. Important because it is only now that the fruits of Victory have become apparent, by the settling down of Parisian designers to the business of creating the new and the exclusive, totally freed from the strain and sorrows of war . . . the lovely creations . . . now awaiting your inspection at this Store.

As the years passed, the annual week-long wingding was enhanced by participating merchants who backed the indefatigable Stampede Board volunteers. For the hectic week, they converted the city core into a western town with horse troughs, hay bales, slab-sided storefronts, street dances, chuckwagons and cowboys, and roundup-style breakfasts cooked out on the street.

Onto this heady scene, about 1955, there emerged a new attraction. Three members of the Calgary Rotary Club (there was only one local group in those days) decided to stage an outdoor pre-Stampede breakfast for club members, their families, and their Stampede house guests. The three were Harry Hays, who farmed on the southern outskirts of the city; Watson Hook, head of a large billboard and sign company; and Ron Jenkins, inheritor of his father's southern Alberta retail grocery chain. These three wealthy and ebullient Rotarians enlisted the help of oilman Cody Spencer, who had designed and constructed some very efficient portable sheet metal barbecue ovens.

On the Sunday morning at the beginning of Stampede Week, this select Rotarian crowd was invited to the Hays farm just off a dusty trail (that one day would become Elbow Drive). There were about eighty of us on that first brilliantly sunny Sunday morning. We arrived at eight in the morning to be met at the farm gate by the three hosts and handed a small "eye-opener" as we walked the dusty road towards the alluring perfume of an outdoor breakfast.

It was a jolly family-type gathering, enhanced by many house guests from out of town who were soaking up their first exposure to Calgary hospitality. Crossfield-raised Harry Hays (later Senator Hays) was a merry, moon-faced fellow who greeted us dressed in moccasins and buckskins. From beneath his old "mountain man" hat were long braids of matching hair, each tied with a bow made from a one-dollar bill. Watson and Ron bustled about ensuring our thirsts were slaked and our plates were filled.

The following year the (Downtown) Rotary Club held its first public Stampede barbecue on the grass of Mewata Park. I was one of the carvers, slicing huge barbecued beef roasts for an arm-numbing couple of hours at a time. Cody Spencer had cooled his ovens, transported them from Hays's farm, and fired them up again for the Mewata event. We served hundreds of Calgary families and visitors on that site before the Centennial Planetarium took over the grounds.

For me, the high point of those earlier Stampede days occurred each year at the intimate breakfast gatherings at the Hays's farm, well before the meal grew to almost commercial proportions. It was the performance of the syllabub ritual that awed every visitor, including guest Hollywood and political celebrities. At that first breakfast, everyone eating at the stand-up counters stopped when Harry announced that the syllabub was about to be prepared.

Now, from a dictionary viewpoint, a syllabub is "a drink of milk or cream sweetened with wine or cider." The word "sollybubbe" is lost in antiquity, but marvellous recipes have emerged from it, and live on.

A most exotic recipe once appeared in the *Illustrated London News* that called for a silver wassail bowl as container.

> Core and roast a peck of apples in halves. Pour 240 eggs into a pewter kettle containing 100 gallons of ale. Add apples and boil. Add twenty-four lbs. molasses, two lbs. raw sugar, and 2,640 blanched almonds, four oz. grated nutmeg, one and one-half oz. grated cinnamon, eight oz. ground ginger, one-third bushel whole cloves, and simmer for two hours, stirring occasionally,

presumably sampling all the while!

The hot mixture was then taken to neighbours'

The 1908 Dominion Day Parade. The 1908 fair was the largest ever held in Calgary to that date. The celebration eventually grew to become the famous Calgary Stampede. *Courtesy Glenbow-Alberta Institute/NA-4928-46*

homes where toasts were offered to each family member. "After the fifth house, toasts to the people and to the furniture as well were often drunk." Or should it read, "hosts were often well drunk"?

Well, at the Hays Breakfast the syllabub was that in name only. This was the procedure: one of the Hays's immaculately groomed Holstein cows was led through the crowd and carefully nudged to stand over a cloth-covered low stool on which sat a large block of ice. The centre of the ice was deeply contoured into the shape of a bowl. Harry began the ceremony by briefly milking the cow into the bowl. Harry and his co-hosts, Ron Jenkins and Watson Hook, proceeded to pour into the ice bowl a concoction of brightly coloured liquid shoe polish, turpentine, drain cleaner, harness soap, weed-killer, wagon wheel lubricant, and other such weird ingredients. The mixture, solemnly stirred to become a ghastly colour, was then ladled into tiny dixie cups, each guest receiving one on condition he or she downed it "bottoms-up" style.

The bravest syllabub imbibers quickly discovered, despite its horrid hue, it was only coloured gin! It was fun, and much merrier than the champagne bottle christening of any vessel–a cheery way of launching oneself and out-of-town guests into the social whirl of Stampede Week.

Electrifying a City

ELECTRICITY HAS THE ABILITY TO TERRIFY, fascinate, kill, cure, delight, master, and serve. When occasionally forced to do without it we are instantly dumb, deaf, blind, and truly powerless, and we marvel that not so many years ago we managed without it.

When electricity came to Calgary in 1887, it immediately altered pioneer life. Actually electricity, as such, was already on the scene in the form of primitive batteries. In 1885 ex-mountie James Walker, acting as a private and innovative citizen, had erected a telephone link between his lumber company office (at Stephen Avenue and Dewdney Street) and his sawmill east of the Elbow River. The voice wire, of course, was activated by electricity. Two years later another unsponsored backer brought electric street lighting onto the scene.

The salesman for this endeavour was F.P. McMullen of the Northwest Electric Company. He set himself the task, on behalf of the out-of-town syndicate, of convincing Calgary business leaders that Calgary should invest in this innovation to a substantial degree. The town had built its first fire hall, and construction of fire hydrants and a waterworks plant were on council's books. Telephone poles and wires were in place, having been installed and financed by Colonel Walker, to carry telephone service to his twenty new telephone customers.

Earlier, the enterprising Walker had financed the modest production of natural gas from a well drilled on his east Calgary estate. The well's output supplied heat and light for the Walker home. Its small surplus was burning in some neighbourhood street lights, and illuminating and heating the Calgary Brewing and Malting Company plant run by Walker's close friend A.E. Cross.

Even with the promise of gas, the business community felt the time was ripe for another modern public utility. On 2 September 1887, when this part of Canada was still the Northwest Territories, The Calgary Electric Lighting Company Limited was incorporated. McMullen had done his job well. Two prominent officers of the new company were ex-mountie, merchant, and mayor of Calgary, George Clift King, and Major John Stewart, rancher, stage coach proprietor, and resident of the old townsite east of the Elbow. Company shareholders included banker A.W. Braithwaite, and pioneer doctor James D. Lafferty, who became Calgary's fifth mayor. They wasted no time supplying their low voltage direct current to the core of the community.

It was a hectic and rather confusing time for Calgarians as they attempted to traverse city streets. Thankfully, much of the disruption occurred during reasonably good weather. Mayor King had authorized the Bell Telephone Company of Montreal to take over the phone network and erect rows of poles for its lines. The sewage system, attempting to beat the oncoming winter, had its crews trench as many blocks as possible, and town council had not granted the electric light installers use of the telephone poles. McMullen's crews must "erect poles for the Electric Lighting of the Town on the various streets, but they must be placed on the opposite side to that on which the telephone poles are placed . . . " This, of course, resulted in a small forest of leafless and branchless peeled stems–an eyesore capable of troubling those who had come west to escape that kind of commercial clutter.

W.E. Hawkins, author of *Electrifying Calgary*, locates that first power plant at "halfway between Centre Street and First Street West on the south side of Seventh Avenue, or just east of the present Central United Church." Hawkins believes that the company's old-fashioned method of distributing low voltage, direct electric current, rather than the newly devised alternating current system, shortened the lifespan of the company.

Conflict of interest was not a controversial issue in those days so Mayor King, a company director, was not chided for granting the Calgary Electric Lighting Company the job of illuminating the town's streets and homes. While it had that kind of support from town council, the firm had a mortal enemy in the Eau Claire and Bow River Lumber Company. That firm had begun a vigorous business that reached from Kananaskis timberland to a Calgary sawmill on the south bank of the Bow River.

The mill dressed lumber and burned its sawdust to provide heat for its boilers, which provided steam energy for the mill. Soon the mill's power output was increased by the installation of electric turbines spun by the swift waters of the Bow. This, in part, was inspired by the Calgary Electric Lighting Company's need for extra power to operate a midtown customer's planing mill. So it turned to Eau Claire for surplus electricity. The outcome was obvious. The lighting company, with carelessly maintained boilers, caved in, and Eau Claire took over, although not easily. Six years of very acrimonious sparring passed before the Eau Claire people won the day.

However, Calgary Town Council laid down some strict requirements to the lumber company for electricity pricing, physical distribution services, and the reliability of its supply. In 1893 the Eau Claire management split off the electric supply segment of its mill naming it The Calgary Water Power Company, which seemed to hint at the company's intentions to veer towards hydro, rather to rely upon wood or coal as energy sources. For years there was quibbling and squabbling. There were quarrels over such matters as financing the uprooting of old power poles and of establishing specific new overhead wire routes to street, factory, and home customers. Nature got in on the act, too. The Eau Claire mill suffered seasonal feast and famine in water supplies, and winter ice floes and jams on the Bow blocked the turbines, creating intolerable power outages.

Still, the Calgary Water Power Company enjoyed a decade-long halcyon existence, having been granted monopolistic authority in the fields of water works and supplying electric current to every type and size of manufacturer, commercial business, institution, and private customer. But the marriage between the privately owned power plant and the town was too rocky to survive.

The only solution was for Calgary, which had recently been granted city status, to build and run its own municipal power source. The site for the coal-fired, steam-driven Atlantic Avenue power house was on the northeast corner at today's Ninth Avenue and Fifth Street West. The plant, providing

The City of Calgary power electric truck advertising its product. *Courtesy Glenbow-Alberta Institute/NA-4477-48*

customers with twenty-four-hour service, came on stream Saturday 2 December 1902.

The months went by and the power plant's load increased at an alarming rate, but fortunately a backup was now in existence. The new Calgary Power and Transmission Company had opened its hydro plant at Horseshoe Falls on the Bow River at Seebe. However, Calgary's population and its commercial requirements, including those of the new and rapidly expanding electric street railway system, meant its needs were mushrooming.

By mid-1910 hydro power from the Bow valley and the steam-generated power from the Atlantic Avenue plant together were managing to keep Calgary's wheels moving. Meanwhile, a tall brick power house arose beside the Elbow River at the east end of the exhibition grounds in Victoria Park. Coal for this new steam plant was delivered on a CPR siding right to the spot, and Elbow river water supplied and cooled the complex. At the start of 1911 the $100,000 Victoria Park electric station took over the job, with peak load assistance from Calgary Power's hydro at Seebe and, later, at the Ghost River. At that point, the Atlantic Avenue veteran was dismantled.

To some sentimentalists the fate of the old brick edifice by the Elbow was sad; yet it was useful to the end. Its obsolete machinery was scrapped in 1953 and it finished its life as a horse and chuckwagon barn until it was demolished in 1972 when the City of Calgary got out of the power-making business.

Summer Magic

AROUND THE END OF AUGUST LITTLE KIDS get that sinking feeling that another carefree summer holiday has slipped away. In my day that was the time for a final plea for a summer's-end picnic at Bowness Park.

The park, a wooded double-island donation to the city by pioneer developer John Hextall in 1912, came into being as the result of a shrewd land and transportation swap. Hextall was starting an up-scale housing development in the western part of the Bow Valley beyond the city limits. He negotiated for a streetcar link between his own new baronial home on the property and the city of Calgary. In exchange he offered the island pair, which could be converted from uncleared ranch land into a public park.

Following completion of a great deal of landscaping, Bowness Park was placed under the jurisdiction of the Calgary Municipal Railway. On a holiday weekend as many as twenty-five thousand Calgarians of all ages rode by streetcar to the park west of town. Fees for use of the park's features took the form of streetcar fares. Right through the disturbed and straitened days of two world wars, and the Depression of the 1930s, the park enjoyed tremendous popularity not only because the price was right, but also because of the amenities. Attendance was heavy, especially on long weekends, and the street railway dispatchers were kept on their toes allocating sufficient vehicles (a streetcar and its trailer could transport three hundred people in a crush!) to handle the traffic on the single-track route.

Our family's day at Bowness had to be planned carefully. We packed picnic baskets with sandwiches, lemonade, citronella to ward off mosquitoes, calamine lotion for sunburn, bathing suits, and caps and towels. A twenty-minute Killarney streetcar ride would take us down to the Bank of Montreal corner at First Street West and Eighth Avenue. There we would transfer to the Bowness car that ran on an hourly schedule. Out in the country beyond Hillhurst the Bowness car always stopped before crossing the river on the Shouldice Bridge.

There, the motorman would pull onto a passing track to await the inbound streetcar. Meanwhile, nearly everyone would surge from the waiting tram and cross the gravel road to a two-storey wooden building where you could buy an ice cream cone or a bottle of Orange Crush or Zem-Zem for a nickel. A couple of blasts on the streetcar's air whistle would send you hustling back aboard. Before continuing the journey the motorman would cruise the length of the car collecting a second fare that he had you stuff into the glass-walled ticket box he carried.

It took the rest of the morning to reach the Bowness Park entrance, and it occupied a lot of the evening for the return journey at the end of an exciting day. Eagerly you trooped down a sloping road and across a log bridge onto the island, while beneath you earlier arrivals, in canoes or row-boats, glided on the calm dark waters of the lagoon. On the right, at the south end of the bridge, was the boat house with a wide wooden jetty along which rested a neat row of upturned canoes and, bobbing in the water, some varnished row-boats. On the left after you had passed the bridge was the dance pavilion and ice cream parlour. Amid the trees further west were some rented summer cottages.

Ahead of you among the giant cottonwood trees were the picnic spots with settles and wooden tables. The more favoured places were those overlooking the Bow River and the Keith tuberculosis sanatorium's cluster of white stucco pavilions with their bright red roofs, and gardens that were being groomed on acres of former prairie benchland. Where you picnicked in the park the chipmunks were particularly cheeky and tame. Mother sent you with a metal billy-can down a tree-shaded path to "the hot water man." Outside his small wooden hut near the outdoor biffies that

Boating was only one of the attractions that drew huge crowds to Bowness Park in the summer. *Courtesy Glenbow-Alberta Institute/NA-1496-4*

reeked of chloride of lime, he had a fire pit over which hung a cauldron of boiling water. It was free for tea-making picnickers.

Swimming was next on the calendar, once a "decent time for your food to settle" had passed amid much impatience. The swimming pool was surrounded by wooden dressing-room buildings and a broad walk of wet splintering planks off which you plunged into the slightly heated pool water. There were three levels of diving boards at the south end and your shouts of joy added to the din of mainly young bathers. Swim wear was very standardized. It was a scooped-neck, cap sleeve or sleeveless one-piece navy cotton suit with a half or full skirt. Most of the garment was outlined with narrow white tape. This cloying, all-revealing bathing suit either was your own or rented at the bathing house for the sum of, naturally, one streetcar ticket, the medium of exchange at Bowness Park.

Later, with crinkly, slightly blue fingertips and toes, and a huge case of the shivers from the chilly water and happiness, you were directed by patiently watching Mother to nip into the bathhouse to dry off and change into your coveralls and running shoes for the balance of the afternoon.

Out back of the swimming pool was one of the park's great attractions, a merry-go-round. Its barrel-organ music had been heard in Winnipeg for many years before the gaudily painted and mirrored machine with its bobbing horses and gilded "coach" seats had been bought for Bowness patrons. That same carousel, by the way, enjoys yet another chapter of its ever-circling existence each summer at Heritage Park.

Another great Bowness attraction was the main lagoon from which branched narrower waterways for careful boaters. Out in the middle of the water was a blocky white wooden building with green trim. On its three park sides gaping caverns each contained a loudspeaker. An electronic phonograph, operated by a young man who reached the building by canoe, played gentle music for those who strolled the pathways or lolled in boats around it. In 1920 (it lasted until 1965) a silvery metal fountain was installed in mid-lagoon not far to the west of the phonograph. It awed watchers with its unusual ability to throw sprays and columns of water in a novel succession of magically changing colours.

Bowness Park had its Lagoon Dining Room, children's seesaws and swings, and a lawn-edged wading pool. In the evenings, big wooden flaps that were hinged at the top were lifted, revealing the fly-screened walls of the dance pavilion. There, with a balmy Bow valley breeze drifting across the dance floor, park visitors fox trotted, waltzed, and jitter-bugged to the music of a local band of five or so musicians, all for the price of a streetcar ticket per set of dancing tunes.

As for those days when we were very young, reluctantly but wearily, holding Mother's hand, we trudged up the slope with empty picnic baskets, swim-tousled hair and tired feet after a very active day. Though I was probably a bit cranky by then, deep down I knew that there were few places on earth more magical than Bowness Park, way out beyond town at the end of the streetcar line.

Milking the Business World

MILK AND EGGS, THOUGH CONSIDERED STAPLE foods, were not readily available to Calgary's first householders. Charles Jackson was the first person to supply milk to the little knot of settlers. His initial source was probably the first cattle in this area, owned by homesteader Sam Livingston, whose arrival preceded that of the mounted police. The two pioneers settled several miles apart, Livingston homesteading his acreage in today's Glenmore area, Jackson putting down his roots on the west hill near the location of Upper Sunalta.

A short while later Jackson, having acquired his own milk cows to ensure steady and sufficient supplies for his customers, broadened his business to better serve new arrivals to the frontier settlement. The main challenge to his enterprise resulted from the eagerness of the newcomers to have their own cow and some chickens. It was understandable considering the skimpy incomes they endured while establishing their own career ventures.

Another rival was Jackson's wealthy neighbour to the west, W.J. Tregillus, who farmed an area along the top of the Bow River valley where Rosscarrock and Spruce Cliff residential areas stand today. There he pastured his fine herd of imported Holsteins. Jackson peddled his milk in the traditional early English style, with a long-handled dipper and a five-gallon can of raw milk. But Tregillus offered pasteurized milk in bottles and, of course, customers flocked to him.

One area dairy that flourished, even though it was rather a seasonal operation, was the horse-and-wagon route operated in Banff by John Brewster. He saw to it that the greater part of his herd seasonally "commuted" between Banff and the foothills, his timing dictated by the summer tourist demand, and the wintertime lack of customers and pasturage. In those days the Banff Springs Hotel was only open between mid-May and mid-September, and a portion of the household population of the town was transient as well.

Here in Calgary the population relocated en masse only once, when original residents moved their families and belongings across the Elbow to be near the new railway station. The dairymen were ready for that, and, with a more assured geographic and mercantile future, their numbers grew as did their businesses. One of them was P. Pallesen whose dairy herd, acreage, and milking barn were located near Spy Hill. In Calgary, off to the east, he had horse-drawn milks carts weaving their way around the city. By 1915 Pallesen was proprietor of the Calgary Central Creamery located next door and twinned to his distribution plant at the west end of the Eau Claire district.

Back about 1884 Pat Burns established Calgary's first creamery at the foot of Scotsman's Hill. For the most part, though, creameries were part of the little towns that ringed Calgary, rather than being urban businesses. High River, Olds, Didsbury, and

The horse-drawn milk carts offering delivery service from Pallesen's Dairy were once a familiar sight on the streets of Calgary. *Courtesy Glenbow-Alberta Institute/NA-2085-1*

Cochrane creameries were typical. Railway service in those days was a frequent and fairly reliable means of shipping perishable farm products. Likewise, chicken farmers took advantage of rail service in the hope of fast delivery of their fresh eggs from flocks to customers.

There was no guarantee that the egg on your restaurant or home dining room plate was fresh. As I recall from summers spent on farms in the 1920s, usually the younger members of the family had the responsibility of collecting the eggs a couple of times a day so that, weekly, several dozen could be hauled to town along with the milk and butter. We city slickers, schooled by the farm kids, would venture into the gloom of the hen-house where all the White Wyandottes or Minorcas, Plymouth Rocks or Leghorns lived. We would move along with our big lard pails, trying to ignore the laying hens' constant grumbling and occasional pecking as we groped for the warm, freshly laid eggs we so tenderly collected in each pail.

Somewhere along the way, likely after World War I, as a house-to-house and restaurant customer service, urban milk-delivery wagons began to include all manner of dairy products as well as eggs. Eggs, butter, milk, cheese, cream, and buttermilk were stocked alongside one another in the stalls at the public market. Of course there were no egg and broiler factories in those days, nor were there marketing boards, although there were creamery cooperatives to help farmers move their produce economically and collectively to market.

Among the physical remnants of the long-dead Cochrane Creamery Limited, that existed between 1911 and the mid-1970s, I came across a letter from the Alberta provincial Department of Agriculture cautioning the plant's operators that they would be eye-balled for twenty-five points of cleanliness. Obviously, sanitation regulations were enforced in those days as well.

I also unearthed a postcard from Banff dated 26 April 1912. With frequent train service between towns in those days, postcard communication was swift and practical. This one was from Banff merchant, C.A. Young, who had written, "Sold out nearly everything this A.M. Please send more cream and milk. Also more butter and eggs. Send butter and eggs by freight." Two days later Arthur Unwin of Banff sent the creamery a cheque and a note: "Please send me one hundred pounds of butter. Here is payment of $24.00."

A very successful Calgary dairy operation back in the early days of the century was the Carlyle Dairy Company, established in 1909. It employed fifteen delivery wagons that fanned out to residential and commercial customers every day except Sunday.

Carlyle's Dairy became the Union Dairy, which, in due course, was taken over by the eastern firm of Silverwoods during whose time home deliveries shrivelled. The successor to the home trade is still preserved in parts of the Calgary area by the motorized vehicles of the Palm Dairy people. The others disappeared years ago.

By the time World War II was on the horizon, No.1 Alberta Dairy Butter was retailed at twenty-five cents per pound, Fresh Creamery Butter at twenty-four cents per pound or three pounds for seventy cents, and fresh eggs for ten cents per dozen.

In Calgary, Burns and Company converted its old creamery into Alberta's first producer of dried eggs. Beginning in mid-June 1942, with the war in its full fury, the plant was capable of drying 210,000 eggs daily. Its thirty workers, during the balance of that year, were able to convert 360 million eggs into powder form for use by the Allies' food industry. Of that, about 27 million pounds of powdered eggs were destined for our war-torn countries.

When I was overseas in Britain, under siege, we received a ration of powdered eggs, which we cherished and hated at the same time. Without it there would have been no eggs in our diet, and we knew farm people in Alberta still had a market for their produce, processed and sold under strict governmental control.

We must have consumed much of that Calgary egg powder in the form of England's insatiable love of custard. The Brits did their damnedest to shove it down the throats of Allied servicemen. That may have given us yet another reason to help end the war as quickly as possible: to get back home to honest-to-goodness fresh butter and eggs.

A Legacy of Caring

THE SELFLESS CHURCH MISSIONARIES WHO roamed this wilderness when Indians were their only earthly companions, were short on medical knowledge but abundantly blessed with survival skills, determination, and a boundless desire to save souls, and, when called upon, to comfort those in need of bodily solace. Hot tea, sympathetic words or sounds, a share of simple rations, sheltering arms, and soothing prayers were their equivalent to the contents of a medical doctor's "little black bag." When Father Lacombe hastened to help the Blackfoot in 1862, there was little he could do but comfort six hundred smallpox victims, of whom three hundred perished.

Our first trained medical man, Fort Calgary's Dr. George A. Kennedy, attended to the ailments of his fellow mounted policemen in a three-bed cabin within the fort. In the 1880s, well-meaning members of Calgary's first benevolent group, the St. George's Society, using makeshift premises, did what they could for ailing civilian settlers of English extraction.

Not until 1890 did Calgary have a proper hospital, created by the strenuous efforts of Jean Pinkham, wife of the local Anglican bishop, and other public-minded townspeople. This first general hospital accommodated eight patients in a converted house on the corner of Seventh Avenue and Ninth Street SW. Its successor, a thirty-eight-bed sandstone structure at Twelfth Avenue and Sixth Street SE, was a very busy place until it, in turn, was succeeded by the larger, more modern 160-bed General Hospital north of the Bow River. The sandstone place became an isolation hospital for patients with serious contagious diseases.

In 1891, four Grey Nuns of the Order of Sisters of Charity arrived here to open a four-bed Holy Cross Hospital in the French quarter of Rouleauville on the west bank of the Elbow River. That institution, still at the same address, has grown dramatically and marked its centenary a few years back.

The first facility to specialize in serving armed forces casualties returning from Great War combat zones was the Ogden Military Hospital, a converted red brick railway company hotel at the entrance of the CPR's Ogden Shops. When it closed in 1919, its patients (numbering 270 at one point) were transferred to the Sunnyside Infirmary on Eighth Avenue NW in Hillhurst, once the Bishop Pinkham School for Boys.

After three years it was replaced by the Colonel Belcher hospital, a 135-bed facility on Eighth Avenue SW where Penny Lane stands today. Then, in 1943, a new Colonel Belcher was opened on the site of the beautiful Pat Burns mansion on the west side of Fourth Street from Memorial Park.

Many Calgarians in, or approaching, their senior years will have been told they were born at the Scottish Nursing Home. Historically elusive, it was

Early Calgary churches and hospitals. *Courtesy Glenbow-Alberta Institute/NA-468-5*

renowned for its maternity program and other medical successes in Calgary's earlier years. Here I must give respectful credit to Glenbow's "historical archaeologist" Lindsay Moir for helping trace the convoluted and intriguing background of that small privately owned hospital.

The Scottish Nursing Home had its beginning at 613 Twenty-fourth Avenue SW in 1915. In 1918 it moved to a converted mansion at 2410 5A Street SW, two blocks from today's Mission shopping area, and between the years 1929 and 1938 was called the Scottish Private Hospital. During the early years at that location, its matron was ex-British army nurse Miss L.B. Peat.

Between 1939 and 1943, the Scottish Private Hospital was run by Miss Lena S. Blackwood with Mary Wilson as matron. Inexplicably, for one year only—1940—the institution was called Ayrshire House. However, when Miss Ada Gossett took the helm for the last years of its existence, the old name was disinterred, and until its demise in 1950, it offered solace for the poor and the pregnant as the Scottish Nursing Home.

Another highly rated private hospital of bygone years was the Western. Its owner was Mrs. Barber, a registered nurse, and her right hand was nurse Miss Creagan. The hospital they opened was on the northwest corner of Fourteenth Avenue and Second Street West, another "medicated" old Calgary residence. The two women transformed the rambling turreted family home into a spotless little hospital to serve about ten patients, with cheerful rooms, and a small, shiny, well-equipped operating room at the back of the house.

The meals were good, the service very personal, and the medical services top-notch. Doctors, vocal in their praise, liked the Western because of its equipment and the one-on-one ambience involving patient, nurse, and physician or surgeon.

My parents were hospitalized at the Western on more than one occasion. It was my first childhood contact with a hospital, its hushed whiteness, its carbolic smell, and strict visiting hour schedule. Looking back on it, the Western was an intimate, antiseptic island, and the passport to it was a frown directed at me, and a quiet voice with a commanding "Shhh!" designed for small noisy boys.

In 1922 that same Miss L.B. Peat, who had seen army service in Malta during World War I, became the first matron of the initial thirty-three-bed Junior Red Cross Hospital for children—usually referred to publicly as the crippled children's hospital. Located originally at 522 Eighth Avenue SW, it was the first of its kind in Canada and was the forerunner of today's Alberta Children's Hospital.

The Salvation Army's Grace Maternity Hospital and Girl's Home, as it was called formerly, took over the old Pinkham school/military hospital building tucked beneath the towering North Hill near Tenth Street NW, opening its doors in 1926. When I was old enough to realize it, I discovered it was the especially sympathetic and tight-lipped place for "nice" girls who, for some reason I was not old enough to understand, were admitted by their distraught parents when nobody nosy was looking.

Many years later I learned of the high degree of understanding and compassion of "The Army." The solid foundation for respect and admiration was well-earned by Grace Hospital as the years passed and its facilities and services expanded.

There is a brief and tragic story attached to one of the more unusual Calgary private hospitals. Dr. Ernest Wills arrived here with his family in July 1903. Alarmed by the extent of tuberculosis and the lack of treatment facilities in this area, he established and furnished, at his own expense, a small tuberculosis sanatorium in his home on Prospect Avenue a few doors from Eighth Street SW.

Frugal by nature, but also out of necessity, Dr. Wills travelled to and from his office by bicycle in those long-ago days when Eighth Street was unpaved. One day in 1904, only weeks after opening his little refuge for tuberculosis victims, he was thrown from his bicycle when he hit an especially bad pothole on the Eighth Street steep bend at Royal Avenue.

The following day, 22 September 1904, Dr. Wills succumbed to his injuries and his laudable dream hospital vanished from the Calgary scene a short time later from lack of funds and leadership.

Our city's history includes well over a century of outstanding development in hospital care. The struggle took us from a three-bed mounted police cabin to today's world class medical centre, the Foothills Provincial General Hospital.

I Give You, the Strap

I NOTE THE DREARY DISCUSSION ON THE USE of the strap in matters of student discipline is still on school board agendas. My recollections of the use of the strap from my public school days are vivid and positive, making me wonder why some people are making such a fuss.

I think it is misdirected adult guilt that makes some people get all twittery, picturing a hulking sadistic know-it-all adult thrashing the heck out of a poor little defenceless, snivelling kid. Obviously they were not even spectators, let alone participators, during those tender years when the kids' ids were supposed to resemble writhing, exposed raw nerve-ends.

As one who "got the strap" on four occasions between grades three and eight, I surely must be an unimpeachable authority? I like to think so for several reasons, principally because my id, after a great many years, is still as warped as ever, and that is not the strap's fault, either! For another thing my parents, whom I admired for their firm fairness, either didn't know their Little Precious was being thus disciplined, or else they condoned it. It really doesn't matter which.

In the three Calgary public schools I attended the strap rested in the teacher's top desk drawer gathering dust for all it was used. When it was taken out and exhibited prior to use, most of the disciplining took effect instantly. The pupil "getting the strap" knew precisely why he or she was being disciplined. The rest of us felt this was no time to run risks.

Our classrooms had a long cloakroom/corridor behind the main blackboard. The teacher-strapper and the strapee solemnly disappeared from sight. The rest of us sat like graven images, listening for the whack—two whacks at most. Then there was a collective sigh. Justice had been served. The strapee, nursing nothing more corporal than a bruised ego (usually it was high time), resumed his or her place and the incident was forgotten—except as a topic at recess that rapidly lost its appeal.

One thing was guaranteed: the misdemeanour never recurred. A sexual note is in order: girls, immediately prior to a strapping, sometimes managed to melt the teacher with such a waterfall of tears as to have the whole thing called off. Occasionally a particularly obstreperous lad would try to "wear" the occasion as a badge of courageous triumph. That attitude did little to impress the rest of us.

I wrote a naughty word on a wall that couldn't be erased. I got the strap. I had spelled the word correctly, but graffiti was a no-no. In addition to a whack on each hand I had to bring paint and a brush to school and, after class, erase the word from sight and memory. There was nothing courageous or triumphant about that, or about the parental scorn heaped upon me when I had to explain why I needed to borrow paint and a brush.

In grade eight, Charlie Alexander, Les Duncan,

and I made a regal parade of the formal morning march into school to the accompaniment of marching music played on a piano by one of the teachers. It was such a blatant mockery of tradition, especially since we were three of the older, allegedly trend-setting students that we got the strap, three on each hand. And we knew we deserved it.

The disgrace was modified by having a teacher who had to stand on tiptoe to do the job. Also, we had picked up (from more hardened classmate criminals) some useful information. The strap would scarcely even sting if you held your hand stretched and rigid, as in hand-feeding oats to a short-tempered horse. Not that the strap ever did anything other than make your hand blush a bit, matching your own shame for having been so stupid.

These days, if the strap must be banished in the name of something psychological or psychiatric, another type of discipline should be brought back. One day in grade eight at Sunalta, Les Duncan and I indulged in one of those dumb I-wonder-what-would-happen-if stunts. Our bicycles were equipped with carbide lamps, fuelled by grains of carbide that emitted a gas in water. The school board supplied glass demijohns of ink, for in those days we all used inkwells and steel pen nibs.

Students in front of Sunalta School in the days before "the strap" became a controversial method of discipline. *Courtesy Glenbow-Alberta Institute/NA-2517-1*

Les and I stayed behind one afternoon recess and dropped some carbide into a half-filled ink jar, corked it, returned it to the bottom cupboard and went out for the remainder of recess. In our absence the carbide went to work, generated a head of gas, and WHAM!, the jar exploded, removed the doors from their hinges, and splattered blue-black ink for about a metre.

Class returned to the mess, had to be dismissed, and we ended up quaking in our shoes in Mr. McGregor's office. For some reason we were not strapped and dismissed. Wisely he phoned our homes that suppertime to report the occurrence in great detail. As a result, with two parents as foremen, Les and I wielded buckets, oodles of cloths, scrub brushes, scrapers, cleansers, and tools–all supplied from home–spending two evenings cleaning and repairing. Our parents were excused from "duty" the second night, but Les and I toiled until Doug Norton, the vice-principal, was satisfied that the mess was cleaned and repaired.

Parental anger generated by the inconvenience and disgrace was an added well-deserved punishment. Nobody was allowed to pay an outsider to restore the classroom to orderliness. Thus our parents learned, as we surely did, the folly of such behaviour. I feel, similar handling of graffiti disfigurement today would be a splendid disciplinary exercise for the young and old in any family.

Only once did my father hit me. I had teased my older sister unmercifully in front of visitors. Sensing I had gone too far, I fled and hid in her bedroom closet. My father ferreted me out and administered a single blow. His hand would have been sufficient but he used one of those very slim bamboo canes from which flew a little felt pennant, on sale for about ten cents at the Stampede. How that single little whiplash stung! No words followed, no other retribution. That was as angry as Father ever got with me and, on that occasion, I knew I had earned his wrath.

He was a great disciplinarian. He rarely raised his voice but somehow managed to communicate volumes if you displeased him. One memorable afternoon I arrived home from sampling bottled stout that had been left in a dark basement corner following the death of the father of my dearest friend. Since his dad was no longer around we agreed to try it out. After one bottle I was "out to lunch." Somehow I tottered home and managed to make my way, unnoticed I thought, to the bathroom.

I was kneeling before the biffy, turning myself inside out, feeling death would be a relief when Father's voice gently intruded upon my noisy retching. "Having fun?" he asked, and was gone. That was it. Believe me, the strap's nothing!

Mounties on the Move

CALGARY'S ORIGINS RAISE SEVERAL CURIOUS points. One story holds that explorer Chevalier de Niverville chose the confluence of the two rivers as a suitable site for an outpost that he established and named Fort La Jonquiere in honour of the governor general of Canada. That would have been in 1751. But the old Indians to whom the area was home had no recollection of such a fort.

Another oddity is that the mounties in 1875 supposedly looked down upon the future location of Fort Calgary from the crest of the north hill. Nearly everyone else, although there were not many in those days, approached the place from the east or the south. In this case, "F" troop of the North-West Mounted Police had been summoned to ride from their base at Fort Macleod to Red Deer. They and Fort Edmonton's "A" troop were ordered to the midway point to be inspected by General Sir Edward Selby-Smyth, the officer commanding Canada's militia.

The group likely did not give the valley a second thought as they rode north. Returning from the Red Deer rendezvous, however, was a different story. This time the south-bound mounties under Colonel Macleod had orders to establish a base about halfway between where they had been and where they were headed. From the hilltop this looked as good a place as any. So they dropped to the valley floor, swam their horses, and rafted their supply wagons atop waterproof tarpaulins across the Bow River.

At the junction of the Swift (Elbow) and the Bow rivers they dug trenches, roofed them with mud and branches, built crude fireplaces, and, in groups of six and eight, prepared for winter.

A building crew from the I.G. Baker Company at Fort Benton, Montana, was hired to erect the fort. The workmen felled and trimmed dry pine logs upstream on the Swift, then floated them down to the river junction. Soon, a one-hundred-man barracks, a kitchen and dining hall, a guardroom that would hold twelve prisoners, an eight-bed hospital, blacksmith shop, and stabling for fifty horses, edged the parade square. The mounties were all settled in time to have a noisy, joyful 1875 Christmas dinner.

Relations between Calgarians and those at the fort were far from cordial. Although townspeople found it comforting to know the red-coated horsemen were nearby and available in case of trouble, they were keen to assert their own law-making capabilities. They could afford only a tiny police force, and the mounties were not impressed by the pair's disciplinary prowess. The fact that several mounted policemen left the force and became successful civilian business and professional men of Calgary did not stoke the fires of cordiality one bit.

There were some prickly incidents when mounties entered the town to make arrests upon the orders of Colonel William M. Herchmer, com-

The Deane house was built in 1906 for Superintendent R.B. Deane, commanding officer of the North-West Mounted Police at Fort Calgary. The house was moved a number of times. Here, in 1929, it is being pulled by a tractor across a temporary bridge onto a new concrete foundation. *Courtesy Glenbow-Alberta Institute/NA-2186-6*

mander of the fort, who bristled at the thought of having civilian cops and a town at his doorstep. He did little to discourage his men from extending their disciplinary activities into the community.

On one occasion police chief Jack Ingram reported to Superintendent Herchmer that the town's jail was not quite ready to receive prisoners. He politely asked if he could use a couple of the fort's cells. Herchmer not only flatly refused, he had his constables arrest a lawbreaker right under the police chief's nose. Shortly after, a seemingly retaliatory gesture occurred when a pair of husky Calgarians waylaid Herchmer one November night in 1884 and tossed him off the Elbow River Bridge.

The most serious encounter began in June 1892 when a newly arrived Chinese brought smallpox to the community. In an attempt to protect his charges, Police Chief Thomas English, then one of the town's three lawmen, hid the sufferer in a small shack on the outskirts of town. This, of course, meant the man was "in mountie territory."

The situation deteriorated rapidly when other Chinese and a local Caucasian carpenter contracted the disease and were also banished to the same shack. The chief and the mounties overreacted when it came to custody of the sick carpenter's possessions, and English found himself in handcuffs in the mounted police barracks!

The trouble was far from over by the time the patients were declared free of smallpox. The mounties backed off, knowing the ex-patients were returning to town. But it was the townspeople's turn to overreact, and they torched and vandalized Chinese property. The mayor was on holiday, the police chief was in Winnipeg on business, and the two constables couldn't handle the mob. Calgary's city council was very grateful the mounties were nearby to straighten out the mess. After it was all over, an alderman urged in vain that Calgary's police officers should be fired and the job given to the mounties. But a new mayor was elected and assumed the role of chief magistrate, a title that persists to this day.

One of William Herchmer's successors, Superintendent Richard Burton Deane, was equally strict but less of a martinet. He reported for duty in 1906 and immediately took issue with the accommodation available to him within the boundaries of the fort. There was a commanding officer's house on the grounds, but Deane felt his predecessor had left it in a sorry state. So he set about having one built more to his liking and status.

When the Deanes lived in the house it was located near the corner of Ninth Avenue and Sixth Street East, facing the barracks. But its life was a restless one. Fort Calgary closed in 1914 and after his wife died, Superintendent Deane returned to his homeland of England. Meanwhile the Deane House was also on the move. The Grand Trunk Railway purchased it as a rail terminal and living quarters for its station agent. To fill that role it was relocated about half a block to the southeast, closer to Ninth Avenue and the river. When the railway pulled up stakes from the old Fort Calgary site the C.L. Jacques family, in 1929, bought and occupied the house. However Jacques, too, was dissatisfied with its location so he undertook a most adventuresome project.

Using steam tractor power, he had the house hauled across the Elbow River on a temporary bridge of log pilings. There it was set on a new foundation just beyond the east bank of the stream. It was such a bold and unusual undertaking that *Popular Mechanics* magazine reported it in one of its 1930 issues.

The checkered career of the Deane House continued. When the Jacques family sold it, even the name was changed and it became Gaspe Lodge, having been completely remodelled as a boarding house. The City purchased it in 1973 and converted it into a centre for artists and authors, christening it "the Dandelion Gallery." A short time later the mounties reentered the picture when its veterans undertook the restoration of the verandah and some of the interior as their RCMP Centennial project. Yet one more change took place. The Deane House was designated a Registered Historic Resource in 1978 and, a year later, the Dandelion Gallery left the scene.

Extensive renovations were then affectionately launched by the Junior League of Calgary and the Alberta Culture and Historic Sites Services. The restless old house had just come under the control of the Fort Calgary Preservation Society, part of the Calgary Parks and Recreation Department. So, with all those new "godparents," and the Fort Calgary Interpretive Centre just across the river, the Deane House, and the fort, stand as continual reminders of that original settlement that grew into the city we know today.

Calgary's Showman

*F*ROM ITS EARLIEST DAYS CALGARY HAS BEEN known as an enthusiastic centre of the lively arts. Home-based theatrical and musical groups packed the little wooden Boynton Hall, and a year later, with the erection of Claxton's Star Rink in 1884, concerts featuring the Calgary Amateur Theatre Club and the Calgary Brass Band were filled to the brim.

The Calgary Opera House, built in 1890, incorporated facilities for skaters and concert-goers. It served the community splendidly until it was eclipsed by the Hull Opera House, an imposing brick building that stood on the southeast corner of today's Sixth Avenue and Centre Street, kitty-corner from the Chamber of Commerce. It became the focal point of Calgary's social whirl. Citizens in their finery attended opera performances, musical comedy hits of the day, one-night stands by globe-trotting stars, and roof-raising brass band concerts. It was about then that Calgarians met William B. Sherman, the greatest showman this city has ever known.

Born in Ohio on 29 July 1868, Sherman joined a circus at the age of seventeen and worked with the Sells Brothers, Ringling Brothers, and the team of Forpaugh and Barnum. By age thirty-four he owned Mohawk Park and the Agricultural Park in Brantford, Ontario, and the Jockey Club Park and Sherman Park, later Sherman's Garden, in Hamilton. Fire was the enemy of his eastern enterprises, but, while recouping his losses, Sherman appeared in Calgary in January 1905 as head of the Sherman and Summer Stock Company, a theatrical troupe he booked into the Lyric Theatre on Eighth Avenue West. That live-performance theatre was owned by Calgary lawyer James Lougheed, and soon the two entrepreneurs put their heads together and came up with new ambitious schemes. But first, Sherman had other fish to fry.

In June of 1905 he leased the Alberta Curling Rink on Fifth Avenue East, renaming it Sherman's Garden, and staged continuous vaudeville performances of the Allen Stock Company. Obsessed with theatrical endeavours, he leased, for the second time, the Lyric Theatre and its neighbour the Lyceum. His dreamed of replacing those theatres with new twin houses seating 1,800 and 1,200 respectively, each with a magnificent entrance, fronting on First Street West at Sixth Avenue.

In the meantime he took over the Hull Opera House in 1905, moved his performances over there from the Lyric, and, of course, renamed the place the Sherman Opera House. In 1905 he bought an exceedingly large old skating rink on the corner of Seventeenth Avenue and Centre Street and rechristened the cavernous structure the Sherman Rink. Although it was on the edge of downtown, Sherman figured it would be well served by a proposed new street railway system, and it was surrounded by an abundance of horseless-carriage parking

Calgary showman William B. Sherman's nemesis, fire, destroyed the Sherman Roller Rink in 1915. *Courtesy Glenbow-Alberta Institute/NB-16-446*

space. (He was right, of course.) The rink opened on 5 October 1907.

The building could seat, though in somewhat Spartan surroundings, five thousand people, with another four hundred chairs out in the rink area for special concerts. The facilities lured all kinds of travelling theatrical troupes, dramatic stars, and vaudevillians. Internationally acclaimed Australian diva Dame Nellie Melba and Madame Sarah Bernhardt were among the dozen or more superstars who appeared there.

Meanwhile, on Calgary's "Great White Way" the Sherman-Lougheed Lyric and Lyceum were doing very well. Among visiting performers were Adele and Fred Astaire, Clifton Webb, Jack Benny, and Stan Laurel. William Sherman would try anything. With the nucleus of his theatrical troupe at the Lyric he formed the Sherman Great Northwest Circuit, booking performances into prairie theatres. During the two years of playing to local audiences in towns of all sizes, Sherman had them performing on a circuit of thirty-six theatres and halls! But in 1911 William Sherman and James Lougheed hatched a finer plan. First they turfed Terrill's large commercial greenhouse off the property on the southeast corner of Sixth Avenue and First Street West. Then they built a unique brick office block inside of which was a 1,500-seat theatre, unattached, to isolate its sound factor. Initially calling it the Grand Theatre, they were able to advertise that it had the largest theatre stage in Canada. Of course that attracted top-ranking performers from around the globe. Sir John Martin Harvey, Matheson Lang, Forbes Robertson, Dame Ellen Terry—they all played the Grand in Calgary with their London casts of actors.

It opened on the evening of 5 February 1912, and as soon as it was leased by the great showman, it became the Sherman Grand, the diamond tiara of his Calgary empire. I clearly recall the "cake icing" decor of the Grand—its bulbous opulent loges with their premium chairs, heavy carpets, crimson draperies, intricate ceiling adornment, and huge proscenium arch rimmed with light bulbs. On either side of the wings were boxes, each with a three-stemmed lighting fixture. A garish fire curtain bearing an English pastoral scene was lowered once during every performance to reassurance patrons of their safety. The curtain also carried a brazen bevy of local merchants' advertisements—a typical Sherman touch.

The Lougheed family had its own private box, though it was used only rarely by family members because of their many other pursuits. When premium modern motion pictures appeared on the Calgary theatrical scene I remember seeing a film of alpinist Sir James Outram conquering Mount Assiniboine. Then there was a slide-enhanced lecture of the ill-fated Scott Antarctic expedition and I plodded and sweated across Africa with Martin and Osa Johnson. Also, for the better part of two years, I haunted the Grand to watch six nightly performances and two matinees weekly by the British Guild Players, our resident professional thespians. One of them, Basil Radford, later made his name with Naunton Wayne in such filmed mystery comedies as The Lady Vanishes. Cast member Gaby Fay later made her mark as Fay Holden, the mother of Mickey Rooney in the Andy Hardy movie series. Gaby's real life husband was actor David Clyde, whose screen-playing brother was Andy Clyde of Mack Sennett comedy fame.

Our house was the guild's second home during their long-playing run at the Sherman Grand. Many a meal they shared with us, our house rang with the rehearsals of their lines, and I know my mother's washing load was consistently heavier, varied, and more urgent for a couple of years. The time came for the troupe to move on with Hollywood as the goal. It was a good change of venue for all of them, too.

William B. Sherman's holdings thrived under his highly skilled enthusiasm, although none exists today. The Grand was garrotted in the name of modern cinema. The Lyric and Lyceum succumbed to the inevitable "modernizing" of Stephen Avenue, and, on 25 February 1915, the Sherman Rink surrendered to Sherman's old nemesis, fire. Before its demise, however, it was an amazing landmark and a tribute to the enterprise of our prince of showmen.

Originally a skating rink, Sherman converted the big structure into a roller-skating auditorium, a popular pastime of the era. It could accommodate five thousand people, for it covered ten city-sized lots. Without an interior supporting post in the entire structure, it measured fifteen by thirty metres and its curved roof towered eighteen metres above street level. Sherman had a sturdy raised stage constructed of concrete blocks covered with maple hardwood, highly polished for public dancing. Next he had the rest of the main floor laid with matching glass-smooth polished maple.

He had his construction crew convert the space beneath the stage into a banquet room large enough to accommodate five hundred people. He saw to it that the fully equipped adjoining kitchen could handle that many guests at a single sitting, and he had planned the year's calendar to derive maximum seasonal use of the facilities. His plan was to focus on ice skating and hockey during December, January, February, and March. At either end of the warm season–April and May, October and November–the premises would feature roller skating. During the balmier months of June, July, August, and September, regardless of the weather outdoors, the huge Sherman building would be converted into an appealing summer garden with the hardwood covered with a false floor. Throughout all but the four "summer months" the large stage was booked for special events such as society and association balls, birthday celebrations, receptions, and small conventions.

Sherman had incorporated a noise-deadening steel curtain weighing over one thousand pounds into his design. It could be drawn completely across, separating the event on the stage from whatever seasonal activity was taking place in the main part of the arena. He hired the very capable former hockey player Lloyd Turner as manager. Turner later managed the Victoria Arena and The Corral as well. When the giant rink burned, the Turners, who lived on the premises, safely escaped the pyre of a showman's greatest adventure.

The Main Drag

CALGARY'S MAIN RAIL-HUGGING THOROUGH-fare, typical of most western towns, was Atlantic Avenue (renamed Ninth Avenue in 1904). Located west of the stockade of Fort Calgary, it became the address of many of our hotels and stables.

After the disastrous fire of 1886, although hoteliers preferred being "across the road from the tracks," Stephen (later Eighth) Avenue became the main road through the centre of town and has maintained that position ever since. For a long time Eighth Avenue's bustle and business included hotels such as the Alberta, Royal, and Victoria, and a host of merchants, theatres, and banks.

At one point, the new principal intersection of Eighth Avenue and First Street West had three banks and a hotel at its corners. Today a few of those earlier sandstone buildings, which arose after the big fire and brought considerable renown to the area's quarries, live on in drastically changed company. The passage of the years, our altered lifestyle, and the remarkable growth of Calgary during its brief existence have all made change inevitable.

It is less than forty years since the orange and yellow streetcars appeared to nudge one another along Eighth Avenue during a rush hour that would resemble a Sunday stroll by today's standards. Their clanging bells and shrill whistles were almost muffled by the clattering automobile engines of those days. Back then the Alberta Corner was the Alberta Hotel, and the Bank of Montreal was of sandstone with a distinctive corner turret with a candle-snuffer cone at the top.

The Alexander Corner, a sandstone commercial building, filled the northwest corner of Eighth and First in those days when the Hudson's Bay Company store fronted on Seventh Avenue. The main floor, which had been a bank for years, became Liggett's Drugstore, a very popular soda-fountain meeting place for the office crowd.

Even that long ago Eighth Avenue was a thoroughfare loaded with ethnic character. Housewives used to patronize the very English-style store of John Irwin, a lordly sort of man with a white apron across his ample front. His emporium was a treasure-trove of imported foods, and the front of the main counter was faced with lidded bins containing lentils, tapioca, and brown sugar, as well as a lavish assortment of British biscuits.

Across the street from Irwin's was F.W. Woolworth's "five and ten" store. Its livery of scarlet and gold identified it as a fairyland of low-cost bargains in an amazing variety of household needs, decorations, and utensils including gadgetry galore. Woolworth's next-door neighbour was Ashdown's Hardware, regarded by some as another foreign-owned business because its head office was way off in Winnipeg! Ashdown's featured a creaky elevator that lurched to and from the third floor encased in an open grillwork of black enamelled panels.

Next door, to the west, was Osborne's Bookstore,

Looking west on Stephen Avenue, 1884-85. The street began as little more than a dusty trail. The large building pictured here is Boynton Hall, located between Second and Third streets east, roughly 310 Eighth Avenue North. *Courtesy Glenbow-Alberta Institute/NA-1075-14*

presided over by Fred Osborne, who later became mayor. Major-domo of the main floor, which specialized in office stationery, was the ever-present Mr. Shaw, an expert in business forms, ledgers, ring-binders, and, for the discriminating hostess, perfumed papeteries. Annually, right after Labour Day, Osborne's was the official supplier of school requirements, jammed for a few days with kids buying scribblers, textbooks, geometry sets, and boxes of water-colour paints.

After the era of street-corner banks, the southwestern corner of the Eighth and First intersection dared to be the first to modernize. With great Greek panache, Jimmy Condon opened his confectionery, complete with soda parlour and fountain, and called it the Palace of Eats. Chubby-faced, philanthropic Jimmy was everybody's friend, and was usually found behind the counter serving ice cream sodas, innovative drinks called milk shakes, and exotic sundaes.

One of the important businesses on the north side of the avenue in the Clarence (Lougheed) Block was the Arcade that led through the lane and the Calgary Market over on Seventh. Not at all like the arcades of today's malls, this was a succession of stores selling woollens, dry goods, knitwear, millinery, and, upstairs, men's clothing. Adjacent to it, even though the CPR station was only two blocks away, the railway had a ticket office, sharing a recessed doorway with Hoad's Cigar Store.

Hoad's had a barbershop at the rear that you reached after passing a brass bulldog with a pipe in its mouth. The pipe spouted a perpetual gas flame for the match-saving smoking crowd. At the front counter near the brass animal a certain amount of surreptitious out-of-town track betting took place, the kind that even had my mother talking softly out of the corner of her mouth. (We could always spot when she came home after having slid a couple of bucks under Hoad's counter.)

Eighth Avenue of yesterday was the address of the Regent Theatre just west of First Street West. It also was home to the Lyric—part of the Pantages vaudeville circuit—and the Princess, which, after 1922, became the Variety. Much closer to Centre Street were the Liberty, the Empress "theatre beautiful" that ended up as the Hitchin' Post, and the Allen, which became the Strand. I have always felt the mall would become more attractive by night if it was possible to see a return of the small single-unit playhouse.

Eighth Avenue's tallest buildings were the Leeson-Lineham Block near First Street West and, on the south side of the avenue but just east of Centre Street, the tall Maclean Block with Wendell Maclean's drugstore anchoring the main floor. At Second Street West there was the prestigious white ceramic Canada Life Building, although it was overshadowed by ex-mayor James Mackie's noble Lancaster Building.

Banishing wheeled traffic from the mall area helped change the entire nature of what once had been our principal shopping place. The invention and spread of suburban shopping centres hammered another succession of blows. Not that Eighth Avenue ever did anything but slumber during the weekends. However, there was a lot of weeknight family liveliness there in years gone by, mainly created by the entertainment industry: motion pictures and live theatre.

In 1919 the phenomenal Allen's Palace picture house opened, followed, in 1921, by the even more breathtaking Capitol. Their garish marquees banished even more of the night, helping maintain our "main drag" as a worthy urban successor to the dark dusty trail from which it grew.

A Close Shave

FOR SOME REASON I HAVE NEVER BEEN ABLE to fathom, one of the more heinous punishments adults can inflict upon little boys is to condemn them to having a haircut.

Blithely, as little guys in stove-pipe pants, we used to chant "Shave an' a haircut—six bits," without being aware of its menace. Never mind the shave—that comes years later—but a professional haircut seems to slash and lay bare a youngster's faith in his parents, all hitherto trustworthy adults, and his erstwhile innocent view of a world that ought to be nothing but fun. I am sure all parents have heard a child's earth-shattering screams of mixed terror and indignity. A few mothers, and surely all fathers, have paled upon learning that so small a person can make so huge a noise.

You get the picture: it's time for your son to be taken to the barber for a "real" haircut. You begin the priming process several days earlier, hopefully working him up to the stage where he is loaded with curiosity and the thrill of a new adventure. Then comes the day when you take him by the hand, and enter the shop past the big glass tube with its spiralling red, white, and blue stripes.

While you await your son's turn in the barber chair you attempt to titillate his normally short attention span by pointing out the features of the barbershop while you try the same manoeuvre by sneaking glimpses of the portraits of the barber's dog-eared 1991 copies of *Esquire* or *Sports Illustrated*'s bathing suit edition.

The barber calls "Next!" as he snaps the hair off the big striped sheet, flicks stray locks off the big leatherette seat, then installs a long shiny board across the barber-chair arms. Clearly his slaughterhouse is ready for your stray lamb. At this point a no-nonsense haircutter will nudge a nervous father out of the way and hoist the now apprehensive child up onto the board. With sweeping gestures of long-practised efficiency, he winds the little paper strip around the small scrawny neck, envelopes the pale child in the sheet, surveys the challenging dish-mop of a head, and grasps one of the assorted tools of his trade.

He doesn't have to touch the child to trigger that unearthly scream. It shatters the quiet of the place anyway because, it seems, little boys are supposed to act that way at the outset of their first professional shearing. Everybody is embarrassed, except the barber, who makes reassuring gestures at the pedestrians who have suddenly stopped outside the shop window, just to assure them no garotting is in progress.

I can't remember personally behaving like that, but then many years have passed since I was introduced to Hoad's Cigar Store and Barbershop in the Clarence Block on Eighth Avenue West. Many barbershops in those days were located in the rear part of a tobacco shop, and Hoad's was one of them.

Along its walls were boxes of cigars, tins and packages of cigarettes bearing such brand names as Turret, British Consuls, Virginia Ovals, Spud, and State Express. There were tins of Copenhagen snoose, chewing tobacco. Some shelves sagged with squat, rubber-sealed tins of Three Nuns and Barney's pipe tobacco, boxes of Corona cigars, fat tins of "roll-your-own" Player's cigarette tobacco and packets of Zig-Zag papers.

At one end of the main counter was a sizeable metal dog with a pipe in its mouth from which perpetually hissed a gas-fed flare. Alongside was a snipper for cutting off the tip of a cigar before putting it to the flame.

Beyond the tobacco counters was a tall shoe-shine stand on which, at the top of three steps, men sat in upholstered arm chairs. Below them, at foot level, a pair of shoe-shine "boys" crouched on small stools, rubbing black or brown shoe polish into the leather with their hands, then making their long polishing cloths go "flick-flack" until the shoes gleamed like mirrors–a splendid dime's worth plus a nickel tip.

The barbershop could be found at the back of the long, narrow building. Backing onto a mirrored wall was a line of five barber chairs, their footplates engraved with the maker's name, Koken. For the length of the mirrors behind the chairs was a shelf loaded with bottles of coloured liquid tonics with shaker tops. Facing all this was a row of leather arm chairs where you awaited your turn. Mother or Father had selected a favourite barber, so you waited for him to become available for the big event.

As you waited you watched, thanks to the mirrored reflections of the neck trimming, the hair singeing with slim wax tapers, and the steam towelling of faces, the lathering, and the shaving with straight-edge razors that always was preceded by the precise "whick-whack" of the razor edge against a long leather razor strap.

High on the back wall were small windows facing the back lane and, below them, a table loaded with obsolete magazines. Framed coloured cartoon-type paintings of gambling games with dogs as card players decorated both side walls. I seem to remember the participants in various contests as including a Boxer, Collie, Terrier, and Bulldog, each dressed in "people clothes," and smoking tobacco.

The hairstyles that emerged from those barbershops were something to behold. The most unlikely men would demand a crew cut (or brush cut)–that would mean "very short back and sides" and the top of the head cropped short by the carefully gauged passage of the hand (later electric) clippers. Those hand-squeezed clippers must have helped barbers develop outstanding wrist muscles. The hairstyle parted in the middle we nicknamed an "Elmer," for it made a fellow appear very rural and, perhaps, a little slow-witted.

Then there was the pompadour, short everywhere but the top, which remained untouched. A true pompadoured male often had to sleep wearing a skull-cap. By day he was regarded as having patent-leather hair because of the shiny slick of scented gunk he slathered on it to keep its movie hero George Raft appearance.

I don't remember what stopped me being directed to Hoad's for haircuts. The job continued to be performed downtown at the end of a streetcar ride from home in Killarney or, after school, from South Calgary High. The shop I went to was the Hub Barbershop. It was on the lower floor of what had been the press room of the daily *News Telegram* newspaper and later *The Morning Albertan*. Large windows, below Eighth Avenue

The neighbourhood barbershop could strike terror into the hearts of youngsters arriving for their first haircut.
Courtesy Glenbow-Alberta Institute/NA-1868-40

West's sidewalk level allowed you to watch the legs and feet of passing Calgary pedestrians as you waited for your haircut.

Now, I wonder if there is some part of people you first look at, to help you size them up? I look at shoes and legs, a habit I know I picked up at the Hub. To this day I try, without appearing instantly shy and crest-fallen, to glance at the feet. I feel it is possible to learn a lot from that glance: if a person has scuffed footwear, how and where the shoes are the most worn, or unpolished, or how crooked, and what type are the heels.

I recall developing that method of assessment as a pleasant diversion while having to wait my turn in the barber's chair down below street level in the Hub. I played a game with myself, trying to guess from the hasty and restricted glance of those legs and striding feet, what sort of people they belonged to. Come to think of it, I wonder what I'd think of me and my feet and the condition of my shoes if they walked past me!

Home-brewed

PRIOR TO THE YEAR 1000 A.D., WHICH WAS a little before our time, there was mention in the Middle East of a drink called "beer." That same venerable beverage, locally made, appeared on the Calgary scene in 1885, a product of the small, short-lived Bow River Brewery run by the pioneer team of S. Christian and J. Patterson.

Nowadays we are apt to identify beer with television hysteria. Far more genteel were local ads for beer back in the early days when Alfred Earnest Cross ventured into the brewing business. He was a Montreal-born veterinarian who came to Calgary in June 1884 intending to become a rancher. He was employed as assistant manager and bookkeeper for the Cochrane Ranche Company before taking up a homestead in the Mosquito Creek and Willow Creek areas, where he became a successful rancher under the A7 brand.

In 1891 Cross suffered a serious appendix illness and returned to Montreal for treatment and months of recuperation. During his convalescence he became interested in the brewing industry. After completing a brewer's apprenticeship in Montreal, and studies in New York, he returned west to establish the Calgary Brewing and Malting Company Limited in June 1892.

The brewery he established in Calgary was a cluster of stone and brick buildings on a triangle of land created by the union (in east Calgary) of Seventeenth and Ninth avenues. Towering above it was an imposing windmill, which powered the plant's first water well. Another tall structure was the barley-storage elevator and, next to it, the brick chimney of the plant's power house. One hundred employees toiled among the vats and retorts, for the thirst of Calgarians was of not inconsiderable proportions.

Busy as he was with his new business, Cross always had time to participate in the affairs of his adopted home. In 1908 he was elected president of the Calgary Board of Trade. For several years he was a director of the Calgary General Hospital, and from the time of its founding, was a director of the Alberta Exhibition Association. That, and his ranching activity, led him, along with three of his peers, to create the Calgary Exhibition and Stampede, where he became known as one of "The Big Four." He was involved in the Western Brewers' Association and the High River Stock Association, and was vice-president of the Canadian Western Natural Gas, Light, Heat & Power Company, the Alberta Flour Mills, and the Western Stock Growers Association. In addition, he sat on the directorates of Royalite Oil Company and the Royal Trust Company, and was elected to the legislative assembly of the Northwest Territories in 1899. Obviously, he had a tremendous capacity for business and civic responsibilities.

As for his primary commercial love, generically known as "The Brewery," not only did it swiftly become one of Calgary's largest industries, it also began to export its products, and was one of the first consumers of city electricity and natural gas.

In my early days, we also relied on the brewery for our spring drinking water. Back then the city drew its water from the silt-laden springtime floodwaters of the Elbow River. During this season, we took pails to the brewery to fill them, without charge, from its crystal-clear artesian well. For years that well, augmented by others subsequently sunk on the property, was the reason for the firm's proud slogan "It's the Water."

During prohibition years emphasis was placed upon manufacturing Buffalo Brand ginger ale, fruit-flavoured soft drinks, and Calgary Dry ginger ale, which, the customer was assured, was made from "imported extracts" and had won acceptance on three continents. The company, they claimed, had the distinction of having become "one of the largest export companies in Alberta." Even long after the country's liberation from prohibition, buyers were urged to pick up Buffalo Brand ginger ale from the grocer by the carton or to phone the brewery at E5681 because, as the labels of the 1930s claimed, it had been "insisted on for forty years by those who know a good drink when they try it."

According to its early advertising there was a brand separation: Buffalo Head and Horse Shoe. Later the product lines were Chinook beer, ale, and stout; Buffalo ginger ale and soft drinks; and Calgary Dry ginger ale. For the first five years of the firm's existence the profits were reinvested in the business and no dividends were declared. The local focus of the operation was a matter of pride. It bought only top-grade locally grown barley for which producers received a premium price 15 to 20 percent above the going rate. One hundred thousand bushels were purchased annually. In addition to southern Alberta barley, the brewery bought all its hops from British Columbia, and materials for its barrels from BC lumber mills. It did its own on-site malting until the opening, in 1913, of the Canada Malting Company's Calgary plant.

Our family entered the picture in the 1920s. A.E. Cross felt this part of the west deserved better hotel accommodation. With that in mind he led a company diversification program aimed at buying small town and city hotels, improving their room and food services, and upgrading their all-important revenue source—the beverage rooms. My father and his architect colleague George Fordyce carried out a number of those make-over assignments in such locations as Rocky Mountain House, Calgary, Sylvan Lake, and Trochu. Cross was able to report that, "A considerable amount of money has been invested in valuable hotel properties. We have opened new territories and have aimed at the betterment of conditions for the travelling public."

In time the brewery and others that followed suit were required to divest themselves of their hotel holdings, but there is little doubt their venture succeeded in improving Alberta hotel standards. For the most part, Cross welcomed the move. He admitted that some of the hotels were a consistent drain on the company purse.

The brewery was open to the public without charge. It offered flowing spring water, rockeries, little hump-backed footbridges over pools, and an outstanding display of plants and flowers. During the Christmas season the garden area came alive again with a display of coloured lights and floodlit storybook characters. For several years the brewery property housed the Horseman's Hall of Fame, inspired by Cross's ranching heritage. It presented historical dioramas with life-sized figures, displays of saddlery, and picture stories of equine accomplishments and activities in this part of the west.

Another public attraction was the Brewery Aquarium, the only inland aquarium in Canada with fish from all over the world on display in glass tanks. Adjoining it was the Provincial Fish Hatchery, producing millions of fish fry and fingerlings for planting in Alberta waters.

At one point the Calgary Brewing and Malting Company decided it needed an onsite meeting place. This is where my family came into the picture. The imaginations of Messrs. Reg Peach and George Fordyce were called into play to design and build a "snake room" as it was nicknamed in the brewery basement. They created a beer cellar with aged beams, wooden wainscoting, half-timbered and plaster walls, a wooden staircase and railed gallery, panelled alcoves, dark tiled floor, very subdued lantern lighting—the epitome of an ancient, almost ghostly, hideout.

The Cross family laying cornerstone for brewing and malting company building, 1907. A.E. Cross had formed the Calgary Brewing and Malting Company in 1892. *Courtesy Glenbow-Alberta Institute/NA-3165-157*

My mother completed the decor with a touch of her own. In those days (1920s), women's carefully coiffed hair was held in place by gossamer Princess hair nets made of human hair to match the tresses of the wearer. Mother, ever the dexterous seamstress, spent hours under a strong reading lamp dismembering and refashioning the nets. When the beer cellar opened visitors could look up to the many beams and corners and spot large, quite ominous spider webs. The illusion, so people said, was complete.

Manly Pursuits

I FOUND GROWING UP TO BE A TIME-CONSUMING and emotion-shredding period. When grown-ups inserted their two-bits' worth in my pubescent time machine, things tended to get even more hairy.

One of the more indelible ventures can be blamed on our Manual Training instructor whose name, mercifully for his sake, I have forgotten. He was old enough to know better–I was not. The time came, in our high school learning process, to recognize the difference between boys and girls. We students had perceived it earlier but it took the Calgary School Board a bit more time to catch up with us. Sometime in that mercifully vague area of grade eight, girls were shanghaied into the world of sewing, ironing, mending, and cooking. Home Economics I think it was called. We, who got pimples at any time of the month, and whose voices acquired a definitely lower, though indecisive, timbre were earmarked for such manly pursuits as Manual Training and Drill. Each week we boys were stampeded onto a streetcar and trundled off to Connaught School where, amid smells of machine oil, wood shavings, lathes, turpentine, and wood stains, we were introduced to Manual Training. That meant each of us could choose to build a phone book holder, coffee table, trivet, or table lamp, from a wood of our choice. As the only son of a carpenter and cabinet maker I should have been forewarned. Perhaps I should even have used my own head, something with which I was reasonably familiar. However I stupidly chose to make a tea wagon of birch. I pictured it as an elegant addition to Mother's living room and lifestyle. It would have one pair of tall spindle-spoked tire-shod wheels and a pair of swivelled casters, two levels of tea tray shelves, and a steering handle.

Mother was wonderful. She said she loved it–angular, misshapen, chunky, its four casters balking at every carpet-edge, and finished in sand-papered drabness. I should never have been allowed to meddle with birch, I swear the hardest and most stubborn wood this side of ebony, but without grace and patina. The class had to be kept late until I had finished the last rub-down of this ramshackle project that bore a sort of antique look from the day I began it.

One of our classmates stepped over institutional traces and startled the staff and the classes by opting for cooking. He created an eyebrow-raising precedent for everyone but his father, a restaurateur and caterer, who welcomed the lad into the family profession. Our classmate, for his part, became the envy of us more allegedly macho types, for he was the first and only one to make his fortune! Food, rather than birch, obviously was a shrewd choice.

My struggle was with peer groups who constituted other classes in the Manual Training category. Swiftly and with apparent ease and dexterity they turned out decorative book-ends, serving

While their male counterparts were shepherded off to Drill and carpentry, female high school students, such as these at King George School, studied Home Economics. *Courtesy Glenbow-Alberta Institute/NA-5063-1*

trays, and planters of malleable woods that readily blended inlays, stains, and polishes. Our completed projects were put on display for a final inspection during which the instructor and other faculty men audibly clucked and winced at my ugly-duckling birch tea wagon. I never knew its ultimate fate, although I am quite certain that after my mother's death it deservedly wound up as a dolly for the garbage cans or an evening's-worth of fireplace fuel.

Back in the 1920s, chauvinism was practised openly and unashamedly in Calgary's four high schools. Nobody ever thought a girl could, or would, handle a crosscut saw, and certainly no boy would shame himself by risking impaling himself on a darning needle or a kitchen skewer. This sexual distinction had its drawbacks for the boys as well as the girls.

For example, in 1928 and 1929 when I went to South Calgary High School, World War I was still very much in the public's mind. So, as a punishment for being male, one afternoon a week, we boys were herded to the school basement where, on long wooden benches, we were required to change our clothes. This was listed in the curriculum as Drill. After much scuffling and grumpy talk we were shooed outside to the cindery, barren school grounds, arrayed in ill-fitting scratchy serge khaki army uniforms.

Throughout each school year, the Calgary School Board circulated these baggy outfits as well as an arsenal of emasculated Lee Enfield war surplus rifles. Nothing ever fit properly, so, encased in what felt like someone else's sandpaper tunic, breeches, boots, puttees, and cloth wedge cap, you were a pretty sorry sight. In my case the puttees, wound around my spindly legs, sagged wantonly during an afternoon of stomping around the field one dusty afternoon per week.

We were lined up in uneven ranks and drilled by Captain Ferguson whose brass-bound lungs lambasted us constantly as we wheeled, stumbled, paced, and changed direction through an array of incomprehensible manoeuvres. Each lad watched all the others in the hope of being able to interpret the captain's torrent of unintelligible commands such as forming columns of four, about turn, quick march, halt, present arms, shoulder arms, and all the rest of that stuff. It had us wondering how the bewildered allies who must have originally worn these uniforms, managed to win the war.

At the end of the school year we had to deck ourselves with polished buttons and boots to spend an afternoon competing with similar units from Crescent Heights, Central Collegiate Institute, and St. Mary's high schools. As a charter member of South Calgary's "awkward squad," for two consecutive years I and my fellow "soldiers" never knew the sweet taste of parade square victory. However, we surely knew the bitterness of being yelped at by the scarlet-faced captain, "All those who do NOT want to serve their King and Country, step forward one pace!"

I sometimes wondered if His Majesty King George V would have been grateful if we accepted the captain's challenge. World War II, still on the distant horizon, might have been shortened a bit. But it was not the spectre of warfare that terrified us: it was the fear that Ferguson might blindfold you, prop you quivering against the football goal post, and not even yell "So long!" as you crumpled to the ground from the blast of those hammerless Lee Enfields—or his incredible voice—whichever hit you first.

All of this, in fact, may be why I'm still afraid of grown-ups.

The Right Stuff

TWO CANADIAN CITIES HAVE A HART HOUSE IN their urban midst. Toronto is one, Calgary is the other; although ours does not bear that official name. Over the years, the Toronto Hart House has been home to the most dulcet voices, and enthralled audiences have enjoyed the classical creations of Bach, Haydn, Mozart, Beethoven, and Brahms in its midst.

The house of Hart in our western city has rocked to thumps, mighty thuds, majestic grunts, and the city's heaviest breathing by some of the world's giants of the squared circle: Jack Dempsey, Rocky Marciano, Mohammed Ali, Curt Henning, Rick Martel, Andre the Giant, Arnold Schwarzenegger. All of those and dozens more boxers and wrestlers trained and worked out in the basement of Stu Hart's house, a heavy-duty area nicknamed "The Dungeon."

The first job my father undertook shortly after his arrival from England in 1905 was to use his cabinet-maker's training to build and install the woodwork–floors, wainscoting, plate rails, cupboards, staircases, doors, and cabinets–for the new house being erected for Edward Henry Crandell, owner and operator of a sandstone quarrying and brick manufacturing complex on the edge of the Bow River at the west end of Spruce Cliff. The railway station and the workers' town were called Brickburn, and the Crandell mansion, "the Boss's House," stood in aloof splendour above the plant, near the base of what we now know as Broadcast Hill.

At the time, well removed from the western edge of the little city of Calgary, it was on property known as University Heights, for that is where the University of Alberta was to have arisen. But Calgary was out of political step with the provincial government and the university went to Edmonton. The 160-acre land for the campus, donated by rancher W.J. Tregillus, reverted to agricultural use, and the dream of a University of Calgary went into hibernation for half a century. Edward Crandell, in the early 1920s, closed down his Brickburn operation and moved with his family into the lower Mount Royal area of Calgary. The large brick "manor house" with its twin gables, oversized barn, and servants' quarters knew periods of abandonment, its empty eyes looking down to the east as the city crept up the Sunalta hill, across the new residential areas of Rosscarrock, Wildwood, and Westgate. In fact, it saw Westgate take over a long north-south shallow that, for the years 1928 and 1929, had been Calgary's aviation terminal, the Banff Coach Road Airport.

Back around 1923 the Crandell place took on a most unusual role. It hosted the nurses and patients of the Junior Red Cross Hospital (which was then located in lower Mount Royal) as they participated in a sports day. It was an unforgettable treat for these recuperating youngsters.

The "Hart House" was originally built for Edward Crandell, owner of the Crandell Pressed Brick and Sandstone Company at Brickburn. Since 1951 it has been the home of Stu Hart and family of wrestling fame. *Courtesy Glenbow-Alberta Institute/NA-2903-17*

Years later an old school pal of mine, Henry S. Patterson, bought the Crandell mansion and raised his family there. The huge Brickburn house gave the Patterson youngsters and their lawyer father plenty of elbow room, riding space, and, of course, a panoramic view of the city as it spread upward and outward. The Pattersons left their mark, even though some of the Crandell property changed title. Today we have the residential area of Patterson Heights and, of course, the appropriately named Prominence Point.

Then along came a cheerful husky fellow named Stu Hart. He was born in 1915 and right from his teenage days had the build and highly competitive temperament of a wrestler. Stu set his sights on becoming a good one, as well as an accomplished all-round athlete. An unremitting regimen of exercise and study brought its rewards, for in 1936, Stu Hart was named Canadian Amateur Wrestling Champion. He then went on to capture the title of Canadian Middleweight Wrestling Champion, a milestone of his professional career.

As the years passed Stu became so involved in sports that he could afford some athletic diversion. He earned himself a spot as a member of the Edmonton Eskimos football team between the years 1938 and 1940. Stu was on the squad when it made history by being the first sporting team to play in the newly opened Clarke Stadium. In the meantime, Stu continued to pursue his first love, wrestling, and in 1939 became the Canadian Light Heavyweight Wrestling Champion. However, his biggest and most important victory of all occurred on New Year's Eve 1948.

Stu was appearing on wrestling cards in Long Beach, California. There he met Helen, an enchantingly cheerful young woman with flashing eyes and a smile a mile wide, a perfect match for the happy young husky from Calgary. They fell in love, married, and began filling the house with children, some of whom went on to become professional wrestlers as well.

While the name of Stu Hart is well known within international wrestling circles, Calgarians got to know him best as the originator and the power behind the television program "Stampede Wrestling" held each week at the Victoria Pavilion at Victoria (now Stampede) Park. Ross, "number six son," produced the series, which ran from 1951 to 1989, usually to a packed house and a dedicated TV audience.

Featuring a succession of masters of the sport, Stampede Wrestling attracted stars from all over the continent and many parts of the world. It somehow became the "accepted thing" that, no matter how world-famous the visiting wrestlers might be, the Hart house was their brief temporary home for home-cooked meals, gossip, and camaraderie here in our foothills city with "Tiger Bell" Helen as their den mother.

The Crandell-Patterson-Hart house appears to be wearing its eighty-odd years rather well. It gives the appearance of wanting to keep its distance from the newer examples of today's odd architecture crowding down the slope close to it. The ghost of William Hextall, the architect, will appreciate that. He also designed the landmark Elizabethan-style mansions of the early subdivision of Bowness. Only a few, including the Bowness Golf and Country Clubhouse, remain. Hextall's landowner brother, John, envisioned a high-quality community for that part of the Bow River valley and Edward Crandell, high on the hill beyond its southern edge, was to be the major supplier of its building materials made at his Brickburn plant. It was a dream that ended with the outbreak of World War I.

The Hart and Crandell families were made of much the same tough fibre, although in vastly different fields of endeavour. At the turn of the century, Edward Crandell fell gravely ill and underwent surgery in the Holy Cross Hospital. The story was reported in the daily newspaper in these words: " . . . he was on the operating table for an hour and a half . . . for the removal of a growth on the bowel and hernia. He underwent this dangerous and painful operation without an anaesthetic." Maybe the staunch old house has some of that tough fabric built into it. I like to think so.

The Keys to Happiness

I HAVE FOND MEMORIES OF A PARTICULAR piece of furniture from my childhood days. It was a grey oak upright Nordheimer piano with a matching four-legged bench, perhaps Mother's most precious possession. Since the house Father had built for Mother, my sister, and I to live in while he fought in the Great War overseas was so small, he had to add a windowless jog or alcove in the north wall of the living/dining room specially proportioned and braced to hold my Mother's pride and joy.

She, a somewhat frustrated concert singer, kept pace with the latest concert and pop songs as they arrived in the local music stores. The allowance allotted to the dependents of a noncommissioned infantry-man didn't allow for much spare change, but Mother was skilled at getting her money's worth and managed to save enough to augment her music supply.

After the war, on her forays to town she haunted Eighth Avenue music shops such as Matthews's Piano House, Fisher's Music, Young and Kennedy's, Clarke's, and Heintzman's, frequently with my sister Mary and me in tow. The sights and sounds of those music stores were memorable. While Mother and the young woman clerk played a sample of the latest tunes at an upright piano behind the sheet music counter, Mary and I would drift past glass cases containing an awesome array of music-makers.

There would be a row of shiny jew's harps, mouth organs ranging from Hohner's simplest single reed model to the most elaborate and expensive harmonica, a double-row job with a sliding rod at one end for adjusting the key of the tune. For me, a music fan rather than creator, the variety of ocarinas was fascinating. Most stores carried at least three sizes of those glazed baked clay "sweet potatoes" as they were nicknamed, decorated with Aztec-like designs.

In a music store's display cases were conductor's batons, ukulele strings in glassine envelopes, choir leader's pitch pipes, and a magical gadget called a Capo (a cork-lined bar with a loop of spring wire that encircled the neck of a banjo or guitar). If slid along the neck it converted the entire output of a stringed instrument from one key to another. In another glass case, enshrined on crinkly velvet, would be a gleaming saxophone, trumpet, or a "licorice stick" as jazz people call the clarinet.

Meanwhile, Mother would be appraising newly arrived comedy songs, love ballads, and vocal recital hits. Whatever her fancy, the young clerk would glance at the score and promptly thump it out with uncanny accuracy and ease no matter what the key or how complex the piece. Once Mother arrived home with her coveted music, my sister and I would stand at her side peering at the score and trying to learn the words as she played.

Eighth Avenue West had a number of music shops including Matthews's Piano House, Fisher's Music, Young and Kennedy's, Clarke's, and Heinzman Pianos, visible in this photo. *Courtesy Glenbow-Alberta Institute/NA-3182-17*

I was never a success at the piano. In today's parlance my relationship with the Nordheimer was not "user friendly." After unsuccessful attempts at lessons, Mother and Father decided our frugal post-war budget could not be extended to encompass nonproductive luxuries. Released from that bondage, I focused my attentions upon a banjo-uke, a hybrid of banjo and ukulele parentage that my good musical ear permitted me to tune skilfully but never to perform adequately.

I saved face by selling it at a modest profit to classmate Jack Christie, and converted the spoils into a pair of ocarinas one of which was tiny, the other almost a bass, plus a silvery jazz whistle, a sort of flute with a plunger. I made such hideous noises with the three of them that the two women I lived with, Mother and Mary, insisted I banish them beyond earshot.

As the 1920s unfolded, the time arrived for us to add a gramophone to our musical menagerie, and I was a whiz-bang at cranking that! I was pretty good, too, at choosing the latest double-sided Bakelite ten- and twelve-inch hit records under the Bluebird, Apex, Victor, Columbia, Cameo, and Vocalion labels.

Mother, it seemed, had a crush on concert soloist Reinhold Werrenrath, who, in my opinion, sang rather drearily through his nose, or so he sounded on our gramophone records. John McCormack was addicted to syrupy Irish songs, and I thought Al Jolson always howled in pain. Lawrence Tibbett sang rousing ballads that reminded me of swashbuckling movie heroes such as Douglas Fairbanks and Errol Flynn. Mother also admired the latest songs made popular by Paul Robeson, although she rendered them in a much paler, contralto manner than he, if you follow me.

One of the legacies of World War I was the concert party. Perhaps, in Canada, the seeds were sown by The Dumbells, a tight little group of veterans who, in their search for a postwar living, turned themselves into a touring concert party. They played the Grand Theatre several times and, I think, inspired my mother and some Calgary colleagues to try the same formula.

The Dumbells sang topical political songs and made fun of the discomforts and horrors of war, having just come out of the thick of the overseas conflict. Their blackout sketches and original songs poked fun at themselves and at society and its morals. They introduced some catchy tunes that lasted for decades. Following The Dumbells's lead, Mother and four or five other eager entertainers formed a group and mapped out a concert routine free of the burdens of scenery, costly and involved costume changes, and a lot of make-up. Their material cheerfully teased local politicians and the community; they also sang popular sentimental ballads, and recited and acted out brief and simple comedy blackout skits.

They presented their program for the love of it, without charge, in Calgary area military hospitals, at community gatherings that involved returned war veterans, and at the newly opened Central Alberta (Keith) Sanatorium for tuberculosis victims. The sanatorium welcomed the performers. Tuberculosis was rampant in those days. Located at the CPR mainline whistle-stop of Keith, on the north bank of the Bow River, the cluster of government-financed pavilions (later named the Baker Memorial Sanatorium) was where scores of patients, in semi-isolation, underwent long, dreary periods of bed-rest and ambulatory rehabilitation under the watchful and caring eyes of Dr. Albert H. Baker and his staff.

The veteran's hospital at Ogden was another

favourite haunt, and when it relocated to the city as the Colonel Belcher, the small musical group frequently performed there.

Mother and her concert party colleagues brought a little fun into the lives of the lonely, displaced patients at "The San." They presented British musical hall songs, told corny jokes, gave recitations, and urged patients to join in the singing. I watched a rehearsal of one of their offerings. A quick bit of padding, a beehive wig, some greasy hair pomade, and two of the party became a ridiculous duet singing the dramatic Henry Wadsworth Longfellow poem, "Excelsior." You may remember the heart-rending song of the poorly clad youth who for some reason carried into an Alpine village a banner emblazoned with the word "Excelsior." Despite a maiden's plea to stop over, the young man clambered ever higher on the storm-swept mountain and later was found frozen solid, still clutching the banner. There was not supposed to be a dry eye in the place at the end of that epic.

There were some hefty helpings of emotions around the Nordheimer's piano bench in our living room. Mother was not above knowing and singing just about every music hall song past and present. Father added his intimate knowledge of everything ever written by Gilbert and Sullivan and performed by the D'Oyly Carte touring company, perennial visitors to our Grand Theatre, as were The Dumbells. Perhaps that is why, to this day, I can still hear Mother and/or the gramophone meandering through "A Wandering Minstrel, I," "Daddy Wouldn't Buy Me a Bow-wow," "My Old Kentucky Home," "Stars Are the Windows of Heaven," and a ghostly host of others from our family's musical yesterdays.

Giving Calgary a Boost

THE YEAR 1994 IS A SIGNIFICANT DATE FOR OUR community, for it was only one hundred years ago, on 1 January 1894, that Calgary was incorporated as a city.

Perhaps it is time to table a diary of our growth. Some dates may be very familiar, others will come as a surprise.

Take population, for example. A tabulation (in round figures) immediately reveals the city's episodes of "boom and bust." The first official city head count, taken in 1891, totalled 3,800. That number represented an increase of 3,300 in seven years! The tally of 4,100 in 1901 showed a very sluggish ten-year increase, but the 1911 pre-Great War census told us our population had mushroomed to 43,700 Calgarians.

By 1931 the number of people had jumped to 81,600, but then Calgary's growth lagged through the worrisome early years of Social Credit beginning in 1935. We did not hit the 100,000 mark until the oil strike at Leduc in 1947 started us running! We clipped the 200,000 mark in 1958, and it only took seven years to add enough newcomers to enable us to pass the 300,000 total in 1965. The January 1971 civic census pegged our growth at 403,300; we seemed to "have arrived." In 1978 we were just over 500,000, the half-million mark. The year of 1984, at the young and vigorous age of ninety, we overtook the next milestone with a census of 620,000! We've come a long way since the days of the frontier mounted police fort. Now, let's put this all in context.

Once the police fort had been established in 1875, and the first white men in the area had been identified as John Glenn and Sam Livingston, the professional traders began to move in. The I.G. Baker Company of Fort Benton, Montana, supplied the labour to build the fort, and local pioneer Felix McHugh turned up to cut timber along the Elbow for the fort's buildings.

The mounties had discovered some churchmen in the area, too. There was Father Leon Doucette, who had been sent into the bowl of the valley created by the Bow and the Elbow rivers and Nose Creek to find a site for a new Roman Catholic mission. His base was about twenty miles upstream on the Elbow (then called the Swift) where he and Father Constantine Scollen had built a little cabin and named it Our Lady of Peace Mission.

In the wake of the I.G. Baker arrival, the Hudson's Bay Company did not take long to appear on the scene. It established a trading post in 1876, the same year Colonel James Macleod arrived to take charge of the fort and correct its name from Fort Brisebois to Fort Calgary. The wood and canvas civilian settlement really began to take shape with the arrival of the first railway train in August 1883 along with the establishment of the federal government lands office under the leadership of William Pearce. Soon, on 7 November 1884, the settlers' new home was declared a town. It had a population of 1,000 and a railway station west of the Elbow. Meanwhile, the track-builders pushed on "up the hill" over and through the mountains towards the Pacific.

By 1886, when the first train from Montreal arrived with Sir John and Lady Macdonald as passengers, Calgarians felt less isolated from the outside world. Teams of plodding oxen and freight wagons continued to haul supplies north and south between here and Fort Benton, but each CPR train from the east brought mail, freighted goods, and settlers–farmers, ranchers, labourers, tradesmen, merchants, with their wives and children–lending character to a community whose future was beyond their most extravagant dreams. Complications inevitably arose as all these newcomers learnt to live, work, and play together. Policing and fire protection had to be organized, homes and businesses had to be built, schools and churches had to be established, and all the community services had to be created, then expanded and improved as town life grew in complexity.

The first white male child born here was the nephew of our first school teacher and was named John Calgary Costello. The first settlers' children were taught at a little wooden cottage nicknamed Sleepy Hollow. The railway built its locomotive round-house a few yards east of the depot. The first hostelry, wooden with a tarpaper roof, Calgary House, opened its doors for forty travelling guests in 1883 even before the town had moved across the Elbow from its original site. The first business directory was written and published in March 1885, nine years before Calgary became a city. Its author was J.G. Fitzgerald, an Irish newcomer like the two Costello families, and possessor of a golden tongue–or pen.

To comfortably digest some of his statements one must remember this was written to lure settlers, entrepreneurs, and investors a full two decades before the province of Alberta was created. There was no doubt that Fitzgerald was sold on the place. He had obviously spent some time in Winnipeg, too, for he could not resist a couple of digs at this other prairie community.

> I say it in the full conviction, which is shared by all who have had any occasion to visit this town, that the future of Calgary is more promising than that of any town in Manitoba or the Territories outside of Winnipeg. The climate, tempered by the warm winds from British Columbia and the Pacific Ocean, which is little more than six hundred miles distant, had already been noted by tourists and strangers as the most salubrious and delightful in the world. And this is no little attraction to the thousands who have found the long cold winters of Manitoba and eastern Canada an unbearable burden. The chinooks, which come from the California sea coast and sweep through the mountain passes, have the happy effect of rendering the winters mild, the summers cool, being of a uniform temperature throughout the year. These are some advantages which are making Calgary the centre point of attention for immigration this year.

J.G. Fitzgerald also predicted that Calgary would mature as a manufacturing centre:

> Already there is a scheme afoot to establish oil refineries on the bank of the Bow. A tannery is to be established by a local dealer next summer, a woollen factory will not be long to

Drillers at Dingman No. 1, Discovery Well, Turner Valley, 1914. Oil, perhaps more than any other factor, has determined the pace at which Calgary develops. *Provincial Archives of Alberta/P.1303*

follow, and it requires no stretch of imagination to picture the future Calgary as the manufacturing emporium of the far west, possessing as it does splendid water power and an unlimited supply of coal. A freestone quarry has lately been discovered within two miles of the town, and promises to be of the best Ohio freestone, and a railway already is projected from the Bow at a point near Calgary, to Edmonton and Athabasca. With these few facts before us, who shall doubt the position which the town of Calgary will occupy in the future? Certainly not the author of this pamphlet, who, in offering it to the public, is proud to think it is the forerunner of the directories of the business centre of this district now, and for the North-West Territories in the future.

This 1885 publication offered a bold, and ultimately true, prediction for the success of the petroleum industry in this province. No small feat when one considers that at the time Turner Valley was little more than ranchland, and the CPR had struck natural gas at Cassils near Medicine Hat only two years earlier. It was not until 1901 that the first encouraging signs of oil in this part of the west would be found in the mountain wilderness near Waterton.

Rich petroleum springs were discovered in the Red Deer country during the fall of last year (1884), on the favourable report of experts sent from the oil region of Pennsylvania, the locations were purchased by a syndicate of Minneapolis capitalists who have formed and incorporated a company called The Winnipeg and North West Petroleum Company with a capital of $1,500,000.

The company has purchased oil mining machinery of the most approved and complete kind, which, together with a party of practical miners, is now en route to Calgary. Other prospectors and syndicates have secured rich limits which they are preparing to work, and from indications shown thus far, lively times in the oil district may be expected this season. The oil is pronounced to be of the finest description, and from its proximity to the mountains and the large coal fields, it is quite reasonable to expect that it exists in unlimited quantities.

Calgary is now the most important centre in the District of Alberta. Its position in the centre of the greatest stock district in the Dominion, its situation in the heart of the richest agricultural country yet discovered in these Territories selected by the wealthiest businessmen of the country.

It is too bad J.G. Fitzgerald is long gone. He would have been the perfect choice for publicity committee chairman of the Calgary Board of Trade.

Kicking Up Our Heels

AT AGE ELEVEN MY SISTER, MARY, EITHER willingly or dutifully, took dancing lessons, which my English-born mother considered part of "a young lady's education." She enrolled as a Saturday pupil at Madam Gladys Attree's School of Dancing located upstairs on the south side of Eighth Avenue just west of Centre Street. I knew it well, for I had to accompany her and my mother while Mary went through her paces with a number of other young girls.

Mrs. Attree was a tall, lithe, long-legged woman with a clear, commanding voice who had a most persuasive, patient manner, a military-looking mustachioed husband everyone called Major, and a large, quiet, obedient son named Trevor. Mary was the swan, I the starling to which ballet-watching brought much pain. Each time the little girls rose on their toes, my legs hurt, for I fancied my own toes stubbing pitiably.

When the class was over Madam Attree would instruct Trevor to nip over to the Bon Ton Market on Centre Street for a Melton Mowbray pork pie. That, we would demolish in the little kitchen off the dance studio. It was a Saturday ritual for a long time until Gladys Attree moved her studio to larger premises above Ingraham's Shoe Store on Eighth Avenue across Third Street from the brand new T. Eaton Company department store.

One year Madam Attree held a Christmas fancy dress party and dance for all the pupils, old and new, and their younger brothers and sisters. I went as a rabbit. My costume consisted of a whiskered mask on a white stocking "helmet." The rest of me was encased in a very snug-fitting, fleece-lined sleeper suit dyed snow white. It had a white puff of a tail, completely enclosed feet, tight cuffs at the wrists, and, for emergency relief, it buttoned at the back all the way down from the neck to the drop-down "lid." That part was secured by a button at each of its upper corners.

Madam Attree at the piano struck up a marching melody, and off we walked in a big circle. It was a most amiable, leisurely elimination march. Finally there were about six "finalists" of which I was one. As I passed her at the piano Madam Attree stopped playing and in her crowd-pleasing voice asked if a rabbit ought to be walking? Surely it should hop around the room? The crowd agreed.

Dutifully I squatted and, to a round of applause, started a long series of hops around the big empty dance floor. I heard it before I felt it! A button on the rear "trap door" popped. There was a low giggle from the onlookers. With that, the other button went. The suit was fleece-lined and this was an indoor event, so of course I hadn't a stitch on underneath. There I was, hopping around the crowded edges of the room with my lid fully down. It is rare indeed to be mooned by a very small rabbit.

That blushingly vivid event did not dim my

interest in dancing. We had a few strictly supervised school dances during my years at Western Canada High. They were held in Mount Royal mansions and on their big well-manicured gardens. One favourite place was the McLaws, located on land bordering Eighth and Amherst streets in Mount Royal. Chinese lanterns added pools of coloured lights to the lawns and trees, and we would hire the best band we could afford. We, the sponsors, invented two "fraternities" because we couldn't qualify or afford the snobbery of the real thing. We had the older I Phelta Thi group, which was a bit sexier than the more beer-minded Tappa Nu Keg lads. But we were parentally well supervised, and to my knowledge, everyone behaved very responsibly.

If we had the money—a rare situation—we would go to Bowness. All through the Depression there was live music out there on the weekends. Bowness had strict rules and reasonable prices. If you could borrow the family car you could drive out there; otherwise it cost a double-streetcar-ticket ride each way. Once you were there, the cost was one streetcar ticket per dance per couple and bouncers politely cleared the floor at the end of each dance. The hall was a pavilion with shuttered sides that could be hooked up to roof level. You could sit at a bench table at the edge of the dance floor with your girl and watch the moonlight on the lagoon.

Chestermere Lake was another favourite dancing place. If we had enough money for gasoline to get us out there on the gravel road we could dance to Mart Kenny and his Western Five, who, for a few years, abandoned their long-standing Hotel

Mart Kenney and his Western Gentlemen provided big band sounds at Penley's dance studio and a number of other Calgary nightspots. The original band (Mart Kenney and his Western Five) formed in 1932. Kenney is front and centre. *Courtesy Glenbow-Alberta Institute/NA-3371-5*

Vancouver gigs to live in Calgary and play at Chestermere and at Sylvan and Gull lakes, wherever there was a skimpy living available for a professional dance band.

It seems that every Calgarian before and during World War II danced at Penley's in Calgary. Saskatchewan-born Jack Penley reminded me of Fred Astaire; he had the same build and a lot of the same ballroom talent. Few people knew J.K. Penley had been a logger on some turbulent Ottawa-area rivers and a clothing salesman in Calgary while nurturing a burning desire to become a ballroom dancing instructor. For that reason he made many trips to New York for sessions with famous Irene and Vernon Castle and Karl Berger.

In "the Big Apple" Jack Penley met a young east coast pianist and dancer, Wahnita Barker. He persuaded her to come to Calgary to run his budding dance studio while he went off to the battle scenes of World War I. Jack and Wahnita were married just before he was "called up" to train as a fighter pilot in March 1918. During his absence she built Penley's Dancing Academy into a Calgary institution despite a disastrous fire that interrupted its progress. Upon Jack's return to civilian life, Penley's became exactly what the devoted couple had intended: a place where a person could take his best girl or even his mother or sister and be assured of a good time.

Mart Kenney and his band played at Penley's and Mart called Jack and Wahnita "two of the smoothest dancers I have ever seen . . ." Throughout the 1920s and 1930s it enjoyed a booming business. During World War II, when many Calgary dancing spots were off limits to servicemen, Penley's with its big band music suffered no such indignity. In fact, throughout its lifetime from 1912 to 1964, Penley's, and that other midtown rendezvous, the Palliser Hotel, were Calgary's most highly regarded ballroom dancing places.

In 1983 it seems teenagers made a startling and pleasurable discovery called "touch dancing." In our young days we had the same, though more inhibited, sexual awakenings. One of the escapes from mental celibacy was to dance. Within sight of peers and chaperons, it was quite all right to clasp a girl firmly, but politely, in order to perform the fox trot, two step, quick step, and waltz. It seems we were ahead of our time.

There were also the annual dances at St. Hilda's Ladies College. Calgary youths who were known to be particularly well mannered, tidily groomed, and decent dancers—nerds is perhaps today's term—were afforded the highest compliment of the teenage social season: an invitation to the annual St. Hilda's dance.

St. Hilda's was a boarding school to which wealthier southern Albertans proudly and trustingly sent their daughters. It was strictly run, and its pupils were dressed in a standard impersonal school uniform.

At the annual dance, though, these drab moths emerged as absolutely beautiful, but strictly policed and disciplined, butterflies. Woe betide the pupil or guest who contemplated stepping out of line. The headmistress and teachers seemed electronically acute to whatever teenage schemes might dwell in the heads of dancing couples. There was something very satisfying in knowing I had behaved so well that I was invited back to St. Hilda's for the following year's annual dance. That was a hard-earned and soul-burnishing double honour for an untrained nerdy dancer who had started out with his lid flapping.

The Boss's Son

THE FELLOW SAID AIRILY, "YES, YEARS AGO I worked for my old man." From there he went on to describe his well-paid and rather vague job amid wood-panelled office splendour in the Calgary oil patch when the boom was at its height.

I couldn't match that, even though many years ago I, too, "worked for my old man." Father had been scorned by his family circle of professional men because in his teens, to his father's dismay, he had chosen to enrol at a high quality trade boarding school in Derbyshire, from which he graduated as a skilled carpenter and cabinet maker. When he reestablished his life following his overseas service in World War I, he longed to lengthen the name of his small, busy firm to read, "R.H. Peach and Son." He believed that a man should depend upon "earning his living with his hands, not with just his wits." For a considerable time that made us opponents, although I obediently served my carpenter's apprenticeship under him. Opulent and indulgent, it was not. I remember overhearing him tell a work crew, "Remember, he is NOT the boss's son; he gets NO favours—not one!"

That's exactly how it worked out. I was teamed with Joe Altilio, a short, stocky Italian fellow. We were the firm's handymen, scurrying from job to job in a noisy Model T Ford light delivery truck. Joe and I were regularly assigned the horrid job of dredging dirty storm windows from someone's dingy basement. We had to see that the glass and the glazing were intact, paint the frames, then clean the panes inside and out, and hoist the storms into place, frequently caulking them in position.

Then, as now, people put off winter preparations until the last minute, which meant Joe and I usually had to work on ladders with stiff, blue fingers in icy winds. One command performance had us installing the second-storey storm windows on the Vendome Block on Second Avenue NW in Sunnyside. Those windows were—still are—very large. At the back of the building we raised two adjoining extension ladders as high as possible, which was only to the window sill. Then we slid a refurbished window up ahead of us, each climbing his ladder in unison.

Standing on the topmost rung we had to hoist the heavy two-pane window into its vertical frame. Then, straining mightily because both of us were rather short, we had to reach up and twist six metal buttons that held it in place. For an instant we wobbled, an arm's length apart, as a gust of winter wind whipped around the corner. It was either us or the window. Seconds later I was wearing a window frame while a blizzard of glass flew around us.

With the most sombre caution we raised the rest of the Vendome windows into place and headed back to the shop with the empty window frame. Father had an instant solution. I was what you called "unskilled labour," paid two-bits an hour. So, you see, it only took me about three

The Peach family at home during a visit from French boy scouts. *(L–r)* F. Leslie, Mary Peach, Paul (last name unknown), Jack Peach, Mrs. and Mr. Peach. *Courtesy Glenbow-Alberta Institute/NA-2139-2*

weeks of my hourly wage to pay for a new Vendome glass.

Walter Smith was another member of Father's crew. Thanks to him I became a reasonably good roof shingler. In those days we worked with cedar shingles so Walter, being from the Pacific coast, knew all about them. He was a thin, dry stick of a man, who spoke only occasionally. He did tell me at one point how, in a heavy Vancouver fog, he had been shingling a roof in Shaughnessy. He was so busy that when the sun finally came out he discovered he had been hammering nails into the fog, and had laid shingles three courses above the rooftree.

Walter was a hard man to figure out. We'd be shingling a straight stretch of roof, he at one end, I along the other. Suddenly he would say loudly, "Errrrr . . . ," through pursed lips, blue from a mouthful of shingle nails.

I'd stop hammering to hear what he had to say, but he would still be concentrating on his hammering. I, also with my mouth full of blue shingle nails, would go back to work. "Errrrr . . . ," Walter would say again, so again I'd stop.

He pulled that routine over and over, and I always fell for it. At the first snow flurry he was ready to return to his beloved west coast. He grinned and said, "Take care, kid. Only don't stop so often and you'll be a damn good shingler." He actually put a long arm around my scrawny shoulder. It was like being hugged by a piece of driftwood.

On Ninth Avenue at about Sixth Street SW there is an electrical substation. When the city wanted to expand it back in the 1930s, an old two-storey house on the property needed to be demolished. I was one of the crew scrambling across the wooden shingles, prying them loose and tossing them in a pile down below. In those prepavement days a lot of dust blew through Calgary, and the removal of each shingle released a gritty shower. As a result, the roof was somewhat like a sloping skating rink.

Suddenly I was hurtling earthward through the air, landing with a painful thud on the old shingles. Thoroughly shaken, I looked up to hear my father saying, "I'm paying you to be up there, not down here–so up you go!" I was so angry as I scrambled skyward that, sure enough, down I tumbled again. Despite the drop, only my feelings were hurt.

"First Grade Quarter-Cut Oak Flooring," a specification for a house, usually meant a degree of quality and opulence. I was given the job of laying new tongue-and-groove hardwood throughout the living/dining room and front hallway of a house we were remodelling on Seventeenth Avenue and Eleventh Street SW. Oak floor-laying is a most exacting and taxing job, for the finishing nails have to be meticulously placed and hammered cleanly every few inches along the edge of the tongue to ensure a floor without squeaks or unevenness.

I worked alone for several days while I sawed and fitted and hammered, acutely aware of the responsibility. On about the third day Father came by to see how the job was going. He found me whimpering in a corner. I had raised and broken a blister on every thumb and finger joint on my right hand. Father gruffly asked what was the matter. Sobbing, I showed him my raw hand. I will always remember his reply, "Why not hold the hammer in your left hand?" And he stalked out.

Within the hour he returned with one of his men and told me to go home. Father and I discussed some of these episodes years later once he had admitted I was a successful broadcaster "earning my living just by my wits." He asked me with a twinkle, "Could you earn your living with your hands now, if you had to?" "You're damn right!" I shot back, and we both grinned. By that time I knew how it must have torn him apart to show me no favouritism or benevolence as he taught me to grow up.

A Long Journey

NO CANADIAN PROVINCE HAS PAID MORE heed to the role and status of women than Alberta. The first example of this dates back to October 1929 when the Privy Council in London made public its decision, through Lord Chancellor Sankey, that " . . . women are eligible to be summoned and may become Members of the Senate of Canada." In other words women were recognized as persons and not merely as their husband's chattels.

Following that "verdict," the "Famous Five," all Alberta women, made this declaration a reality. The quintet's dogged pursuit of an official decision, finally enunciated by the highest court in the land, was based upon a very simple question, "Does the word 'person' in Section 24 of the British North America Act include female persons?" Famous pace-setters they were indeed: Henrietta Muir Edwards, Nellie McClung, Louise McKinney, Emily Murphy, and Irene Parlby.

Emily Murphy of Edmonton had become the British Empire's first woman magistrate, closely followed by Calgarian Alice Jamieson whose appointment underlined the huge jump in progress for Canadian women. The power behind the achievement was author Janie Canuck who, in reality, was Emily Murphy. At her side was Henrietta Muir Edwards, an artist and journalist formerly of Montreal. Louise McKinney won a provincial seat for the constituency of Claresholm, thus becoming the first woman ever to be elected to a provincial legislature in the British Empire and Canada.

Then there was "Windy Nellie" McClung, who had lived in several parts of Canada, including Calgary, and was called everything from a "Holy Terror" to a "Hyena in Petticoats," respectfully regarded by some, derisively by other colleagues when she served as an MLA in the provincial House in Edmonton. Another Alberta legislator at the time was English-born Irene Marryat Parlby, wife of the owner of the Dartmoor Ranch near Alix, Alberta. Fluent in French and German, and an accomplished pianist, Irene Parlby soon became visibly and audibly influential in women's causes. She helped form the United Farm Women of Alberta and was elected its first president. Having successfully run for public office in the Lacombe provincial riding, Mrs. Parlby became the second woman in the British Empire to hold a cabinet post. For part of her fourteen years in the Alberta legislature she was minister without portfolio.

Women such as these set an exciting and challenging example for other women as the years passed. This they did despite smug comments such as that published by John Blue, Alberta's provincial historian, in 1924:

> The women of Alberta are well represented in all national organizations for women . . . they have a genius for organization. The women (of

Alberta) participate in a greater degree in the economic and political life of the province than in most provinces of Canada, and are rapidly taking their places beside the men in the conduct of public affairs. Their position depends entirely upon their desire to embrace their opportunities and train themselves for their waiting responsibilities.

That was typical of the gratuitous attitude of men in public life at that time.

There was no doubt that, at that stage in the province's short history, women had made some mileage along the road leading to the achievement of equal status. One notable example of a traveller on this frustrating journey was Maude Riley, a distinguished Calgarian who worked tirelessly among us in the 1917–63 period of our city's history.

A schoolteacher by profession, Maude Riley was the wife of Harold William Hounsfield Riley, provincial secretary, and Calgary alderman and commissioner. She shared the community prestige of the Riley family whose public-minded activities left their name upon one of our oldest parks and districts, Hillhurst's Riley Park, and the North Hill's residential area of Hounsfield Heights. Certainly she had married into a family renowned for its members'

Eight-year-old Marvin Crump presents Maude Riley with a bouquet of roses, 23 April 1957. Hundreds of Calgary children were involved in the activities of Child Welfare Week sponsored by the Alberta Council on Child and Family Welfare. Mrs. Riley served on the council for forty-six years and was re-elected president thirty-two times. *Courtesy Glenbow-Alberta Institute/NA-2864-3044 (per) F*

many public roles. Her father-in-law, Ezra Hounsfield Riley, had been twice elected a member of the provincial legislative assembly for the riding of Gleichen. In that capacity, in 1910, he had resigned as a well-publicized gesture of protest against Lieutenant Governor Rutherford's cavalier and unilateral selection of Premier Clifford Sifton as his successor.

Acting in her own right as a member of a family well-established in Alberta's public life, Maude Riley was acutely aware of the lack of family services in Calgary. So, in 1917, she and other prominent local women launched the Calgary Playgrounds Association. As a leader of that group Mrs. Riley extended its field of interest to create an ongoing program of public service undertaken by her newer creation unique to this province, The Alberta Council on Child and Family Welfare.

Maude Riley devoted forty-six years of volunteer service to that council, being reelected thirty-two times as its president! The extent of her selfless dedication was recognized by her fellow Calgarians, who saw to it that Maude Riley was named Citizen of the Year in 1946, and a recipient of the King George VI Coronation Medal "for outstanding Family Social Service work."

The Playgrounds Association provided supervision of city playgrounds by trained personnel. The program was so successful it was disbanded in 1921 and taken over by the Child Welfare Council as a public service. The first Child Welfare Week was held in 1918. Among the undertakings enunciated at the time were that a child had the right to be medically well treated, well housed, well fed, and well taught.

The Alberta Council on Child and Family Welfare was breaking new ground among all the provinces of Canada. It ensured that a pre-school and baby clinic was made available to the youngest members of Alberta's population, that their mothers were made aware of nutritional requirements and benefits, and that funds were made available to mothers who were victims of unemployment and family crises to enable them to provide a well-balanced diet for their children. Following that, it took eight years of constant lobbying and petitioning to have the city's Children's Aid Department separated from the Relief Department. This created a proper focus for those family women who so desperately needed adequate and dignified services for their youngsters as well as recognition of their own important role in the province and the city.

There have been many changes dictated by changing times, standards, and mores, in a succession of attempts to keep Alberta families and their homes together.

Nearly thirty years ago, on an anniversary of Child Welfare Week, the premier of the province, the Honourable Ernest C. Manning, called for greater efforts to stabilize our province's families, saying, "The full power of any nation toward settlement of the world's dangers can only be directed unerringly if that nation has succeeded in establishing a solid foundation for the family units within itself." On that same occasion the Honourable John J. Bowlen, lieutenant governor of Alberta, said, "The leadership of tomorrow is largely dependent upon the children of today, and the importance of ethical, physical, and mental care for all children cannot be over-emphasized."

Women of vision and determination, such as Maude Riley, can be credited with improving the lives of us all by caring enough to make this a better world for our children.

Calgary's Birthplace

ON 11 AUGUST 1883 THE CPR'S "FRONT TRAIN," bringing tracklayers and their equipment, reached the end of steel on the east bank of the Elbow River. Locomotive No. 83 stood hot and steamily panting near the southern edge of a cluster of wooden and canvas shelters on the western edge of the wilderness. That array of scattered buildings sheltered our first Calgarians. The settlement, in due course, would become known as Inglewood, Calgary's birthplace community.

By the time the Elbow River was bridged and trains were able to steam a couple of miles closer to the mountains, those initial settlers were busily exchanging ideas on the growth of the new town of Calgary. Over the river to the west was the mounted police fort, but on their side of the Elbow they envisioned a Hudson's Bay post, shops, offices, and homes that would form the nucleus of the community. Colonel James Walker, who had just left the ranks of the mounties to try his luck as a businessman, had a small lumber mill upstream on the Bow River.

Soon he was using the stream to carry the logs he milled into structural timber at his plant, which had been erected on a piece of scythe-shaped land bordered by the Elbow and Bow rivers. Impatient settlers and entrepreneurs, eager to erect permanent homes and businesses, created a ready market for the output of his mill.

Things had moved quickly. Back in 1883, when one of Walker's mill-hands, Frank White, had climbed the hill above the north bank of the Bow and looked down on the entire settlement, he saw a mounted police fort, sixteen log and canvas shacks, and nine Indian teepees. But the arrival of the railway changed all that. Before long rancher-turned-brewer A.E. Cross had built a home for himself and family. So had Dr. Andrew Henderson, who built close to the new Hudson's Bay post. Messrs. Van Wart and Freeze, who had been New Brunswick neighbours, erected a general store, and Major John Stewart, owner of Section Fourteen had built on what, today, is New Street backing onto the Bow. Scottish-born George Murdoch, a harness and saddle maker who was to become Calgary's first mayor, also arrived to open up shop.

But the railway had a surprise up its sleeve. Instead of building its station east of the Elbow opposite St. George's Island, as everyone had anticipated, the CPR plunked down a wheelless boxcar well beyond the Elbow's west bank and announced that would be Calgary's railway station. When the Elbow froze solidly that winter a pair of churches, some wooden homes and businesses, a hotel, (along with some very disappointed and financially crippled real estate firms) had to be skidded over the ice west to Section Fifteen where the trains were stopping, a location that had been the mounted police garrison's horse pasture.

James Bannerman was among those who had

no choice but to relocate his business, a well-established flour and seed store. His premises also housed the post office. Rumour had it the railway had pressured him into moving promptly; a post office surely would stimulate Section Fifteen land sales. Left behind on Section Fourteen, known as the Denny Estate, were some fine large permanent homes and the sandstone brewery. But the triumph of the railway-owned Canada North West Land Company was matched by the angry stubbornness of those who had spurned the move.

They didn't realize it at the time, but, in truth, they were the "blood and guts" of what became the very proud district of Inglewood. Although the community has seemed doomed to extinction from time to time, its resilience has helped it overcome many obstacles. Inglewood still has a sizeable stretch of lovely riverbank, a proximity to downtown that is immensely important these days, some very fine woodland, a fish hatchery, and a disproportionate amount of Calgary history, for which we may be thankful.

Its boundaries are a seemingly careless jumble reaching between Eighth Street and Seventeenth Street west to east, then, in a limited way, to Thirtieth Avenue and Seventeenth Street. The Bow River has shaped its boundaries for a considerable distance while, at the same time, giving it some interesting and varied shoreline. The railways, however, have warped its shape mercilessly. Its main east to west artery is Ninth Avenue, which is now, very appropriately, reclaiming its historic Atlantic Avenue name. New Street is one of its oldest, a residential riverbank whose back yards once trembled to the rumbling of trains of the Grand Trunk, Canadian Northern, and Canadian National systems. Inglewood still lives alongside the very busy tracks of the CPR.

Industrialization has been central to the development of Inglewood during every year of its harried existence. In 1902, when Calgary had a population of about five thousand, the area commonly referred to as East Calgary had thirty-seven homes, the CPR's small Alyth shops, and the brewery owned by A.E. Cross (hence the areas's nickname, "Brewery Flats"). Over the next seven years that part of boomtown Calgary had a soap factory, an iron works, two flour mills, a tannery, an oil depot, and a cement plant. The roster of factories threatened to alter the original residential character of the community, especially in later years when a greatly expanded oil depot, a large gravel excavation and grinding business, a truck and wagon body manufacturer, a box factory, a hotel, an abattoir, and a host of smaller plants were based there. That proliferation troubled many long-time resident railway workers who enjoyed the quiet convenience of being able to walk to work.

The area enveloped the Pearce Estate, named for land czar William Pearce, who built a lavish fifteen-room sandstone mansion within the crook of the Bow River, which he delightedly named "Bow Bend Shack." Nearby was the wooded riverbank estate of James Walker, where Calgary's first natural gas producing well was drilled. The Inglewood Bird Sanctuary, founded by George Pickering in 1926 and supervised by him for twenty-six years, now thrives there. The community even adopted as its own the Walker mansion's name of Inglewood.

At the western end of what became known as Inglewood was the Mills Estate, another pioneer property. As the sandstone quarries of Calgary began turning out building blocks, there arose at either end of Ninth Avenue a pair of sandstone schools: Alexandra School, opened in 1908,

When the CPR plunked its first station, a wheelless boxcar, down on Section Fifteen it surprised residents by choosing a location on the west bank of the Elbow rather than the east. Pictured in front of that first station are: *(l–r)* R.G.C. Marsh, CPR station agent; W.T. Ramsay, land agent; T.B. Braden, *Calgary Herald;* G.E. Jacques, watchmaker; Special Const. Fay of the CPR. *Courtesy Glenbow-Alberta Institute/NA-659-18.*

replaced the original East Ward School, and, at the east end, Colonel Walker School, built in 1912. The latter was used as a temporary technical instruction centre for World War I veterans, the birthplace of today's SAIT.

In 1918, Henry M. Jenkins established Canada's first cash-and-carry grocery store, along the stretch of Ninth Avenue. The Inglewood district once had its own whistle stop at the point where the CPR line curved northward to head for Edmonton. It was given a rather eccentric name by a pioneer real estate man and funeral director named Graham. He left his mark there as he had on a southeast residential district by lending his name to both places, except he spelt it backwards. The Cushing brothers' sprawling sash and door factory was also located near the east end of Ninth, and across the avenue sat the glassed expanse of Terrill's floral greenhouse.

At 1030 Ninth Avenue was a two-storey red brick fire hall. When it was built in 1906 a group of settlers, the Thistles, flooded the field next to it for wintertime curling. Today it is a restaurant, but in my pre-teen days it was No. 3 Fire Hall. Directly across the street was a paddock surrounded by a pole fence, the home of four big fire horses. When an alarm bell would clamour, any approaching East Calgary streetcar and road traffic would halt as the horses, hustled by a fireman, trotted across the avenue. Without any direction, the teams would then back between the shafts of their particular fire engine. Harnesses were dropped on them from hangers on the ceiling, and in a trice the rigs would race out of the building and off to the fire. It was always a thrill to be passing by when the firm alarm bell clanged.

Inglewood also was home to Alberta's first automatic telephone exchange. The double-walled structure at 1311 Ninth Avenue East (now a community centre) maintained a steady year-round temperature to protect the delicate new equipment. As the equipment aged, every now and then some relays would stick, stalling phone calls. Rather than having AGT send a maintenance technician, passing taxi drivers, alerted by radio, were asked to pause for a moment to dash in to "bat" a relay into action.

Inglewood's theatre is another distinctive oldtimer. It was the Hyland at one time, at another, it specialized in showing ethnic films. Now it bustles anew as Sharon Pollock's live theatrical playhouse.

Venerable Inglewood has proven it is a survivor, a "pensioner." Its residents and the Heritage Canada Main Street Program have displayed renewed enthusiasm and energy for preserving its heritage. It is a worthy recipient of their attention.

For Ever Piping Songs

A SURPRISING NUMBER OF PEOPLE CONFESS to getting prickles at the back of the neck when they hear bagpipes. I feel the same about pipes, but of a different kind. What makes my hackles rise—in awe rather than anger—is the huge, pulsating sound of pipe organ music.

My first encounter with organ music occurred at an early age, and it was anything but awesome. In the original, tiny St. Martin's church on Twenty-second Avenue and Twenty-eighth Street SW, I became an eager churchgoer for a short time when I was willingly drafted to pump the organ for Rev. Wilford's Sunday morning service. Out of sight of the congregation, sandwiched between the altar and the wheezy little pipe organ, I pumped a handle back and forth, my prowess being gauged by how well I maintained the position of a red marker on a scale. If—unforgivably—I permitted the marker to drop, the organ would react with hints of strangulation. If I overdid it, the organ whined in an octave of pain. The audible reaction from the congregation, the instrument, and the iron-faced woman at the keyboard was enough to make me renew my efforts to turn in a truly mighty performance.

An organ that seldom failed to turn out a performance that was anything but mighty belonged to the newly opened Capitol Theatre. During screenplay intermission Cecil Kappey turned out tunes with considerable vigour. Most of our local movie houses made do with a piano in the pit that provided mood music to match the excitement on the silver screen directly above. If many of our Calgary pianists walked with their eyes steadfastly cast heavenwards, it came from having to crank their necks at every performance to make sure their racing octaves were keeping pace with the galloping posse up there on the silent screen.

The advent of talking pictures, of course, threw many pit pianists out of work, and, I suspect, a number of them became church organists. Most of our local churches had organs that nourished the ecclesiastical mood by thunderously urging Christian soldiers to march as to war. Few Calgary homes had a pump organ, operated by hand or pedal, although some pioneers managed to haul their treasured instruments as tenderly as possible out here to the frontier.

The wife of early grocer John Irwin recalled that her childhood home near the Bow River east of Centre Street contained a pump organ as a parlour centrepiece. Her parents had carted it here from eastern Canada before the railway reached this far west. In later years, local lumberman and musician Jim Davidson bought the Regent Theatre pipe organ when the old movie house was demolished. He installed the instrument in his large Royal Avenue home where he could play to his heart's content.

One of the truly old Calgary organs began its life in a Lutheran church in Ontario in the 1880s. In 1905 it was brought west to provide hymn music for a Winnipeg Lutheran church, then continued on to Calgary where it was rebuilt and later reentered service in 1967 at Ascension Lutheran in northeast Calgary.

Another oldie is the seventy-six-year-old, Quebec-built Casavant, active sixty-seven years after its creation at the church of St. John the Evangelist on Eighth Avenue East, where Calgary began. The church was built on land worth $350 and dedicated by the Rt. Rev. Cyprian Pinkham, Calgary's first Anglican bishop, in 1907. One of the first victims of Calgary's move west of the Elbow (to be near the CPR station) was St. John's. It had been built to ease the pressure on the pro-Cathedral west of the river created by the growing number of local Church of England parishioners. However, when the town centre moved west of the Elbow, St. John's faced an almost constant shortage of congregation and funds.

Pipe organs have been an integral part of many of our houses of worship. Pictured here is the organ and pulpit of the Grace Presbyterian Church, 1913-15. *Courtesy Glenbow-Alberta Institute/NA-4899-2*

The organ, built in 1912, cost fifteen thousand dollars—a huge sum in those days. At the time, it was the largest in western Canada and required a considerable amount of space in the new church. Eight years later, thanks to the unremitting efforts of the women in the congregation, the organ was paid for in full.

By 1950, after years of constant use, the organ was in need of a major upgrading, but the job was postponed for years because of a lack of funds. To the fundraisers' dismay, by the 1980s the repair estimate had risen to forty-five thousand dollars. However, with the help of a provincial government grant the organ was rebuilt. The rejuvenated electro-pneumatic Casavant Opus 492 retains its position as one of the finest organs in Alberta and continues to add to the special ambience at St. John's.

The pipe organ of a neighbourhood Inglewood church, Trinity United, did not fare as well. Including an organ had doubled the building costs when the church was erected in 1913. This made the fire that destroyed the instrument eight years later a bitter pill to swallow.

Back in the 1930s, the organ at Christ Church in Elbow Park was called upon to perform an extra task. With Cecil Kappey at the keyboard and Elbow Park vicar George Luxton (later Bishop of Rupert's Land) at the microphone, *The Vesper Hour,* a contemplative program of uplifting words and pipe organ music, became a popular weekly CFAC radio presentation. As an eager teenage would-be broadcaster, I talked the station manager into letting me "ride gain" (oversee the volume level) of the remote control equipment at the chancel steps.

A combination of outstanding acoustics and a "mighty" organ have endeared the Cathedral Church of the Redeemer to many musicians. The Calgary Philharmonic has performed there, as have many visiting choirs, theatrical groups, and CBC radio instrumental and vocal recital series.

In recent years aged pipe organs have required frequent upgrading to allow them to compete with their electronic successors. Despite this, the breath of the pipe organ has remained a vibrant and living part of many of our houses of worship.

New granddaddy of them all, of course, is the Casavant pipe organ known to its St. Hyacinthe, Quebec, makers as Opus 3623. This 6,008-pipe organ, acoustically designed and installed especially for the Jack Singer Hall, is a thrilling part of the Calgary Centre for the Performing Arts. Ancient and traditional in principle, and custom-built by the century-old Canadian firm, this giant instrument embraces such modern components as transistors and is technically labelled an electro-pneumatic pipe organ. This organ is the reason behind our city's plan to host an International Organ festival here every four years. Would that the poet John Keats could be with us then to hear the music of his words, "For ever piping songs for ever new."

Scouting for Murderers

WE HAVE BECOME ACCUSTOMED TO THE hefty percentage of crime that makes up a large part of our daily news. In simpler, more tolerant times, a local homicide was rare enough to create quite a stir, arousing the entire community of Calgary. Even back then, our city's police force, tiny in comparison with today's, was efficient and determined to solve whatever crimes came its way.

Then, as today, the police occasionally found it necessary to involve local citizens in their fight against crime. One such event took place in the 1920s when a carefully selected group of boy scouts from various troops were asked by the police to obtain parental permission to participate in a manhunt. A local taxi driver was missing and believed to have been a victim of foul play in southwest Calgary. The largely uninhabited area consisted of prairie and bush land.

One warm Saturday morning at ten o'clock, about fifteen of us, each with his water flask and a sandwich, assembled at the top of the Seventeenth Avenue hill for a police briefing. Only the police had permission to enter private property such as chicken coops, garages, and fenced vegetable patches. We were to space ourselves in an east-west straight line and walk south to the river. Uniformed police officers with their holstered revolvers were scattered along the strung-out line.

In those days, that entire area was empty except for a handful of isolated cottages out on the prairie. The area near the Elbow valley was bush land. Hearts thumped wildly as we approached every property, every patch of tall prairie grass, and, later, the heavy growth of bush. It was a heady role for us teenagers, each of us obviously devoid of compassion, yet totally unprepared to encounter anything grisly.

Suddenly, about a quarter-mile short of the river, the second boy on my right stopped and shouted. There was an instant stampede of adults and many shouts of "Stand Back!" and "Hold Your Places!" The murdered taxi driver was there all right. For us, the anticlimax was hard to accept. While it was true there was a certain shared triumph in having been selected for such rare adventure, I felt a sense of deep disappointment that I had missed being the one to find the body.

A few years later, Calgarians were shocked by the murder of another taxi driver. This time the crime was tackled by the Alberta Provincial Police, nicknamed "The Mounties in Blue." Between 1 March 1917 and 1 April 1932, this provincial police force handled town and rural policing. Many of the force's members were ex-mounties and the APP uniform strongly resembled that of the red-coated "horsemen."

A twenty-eight-year-old cabbie named Ernest Midwinter, a native of Wimbledon, England, had been a driver for Bennett's Fifty-Cent Taxi for about fourteen months. He answered a call from the

Calgary's boy scouts were involved in many community activities. At one point the local police even called upon some of the older scout members to assist in a manhunt. This group of scouts was photographed at Christ Church in 1920. *Courtesy Glenbow-Alberta Institute/NA-2732-6*

Shamrock Hotel at the edge of the stockyards at eleven o'clock on the night of Saturday 16 August 1930. He arrived to find four men waiting outside the hotel. They wanted him to drive them to Okotoks. In accordance with company rules, Midwinter phoned the taxi office and proprietor Percy Bennett okayed the job, cautioning him, "See that they have money, go slow, and check your gas." Even though he had followed all the rules, this was to be Midwinter's last run.

The vehicle had plenty of fuel, and Midwinter was carrying only $15.50 of the company's money. Three of the fares got into the back seat, the fourth sat beside the driver. They drove in silence through Midnapore, and near DeWinton (the road went through there in the old days) one of the back-seat passengers asked the driver to stop. Suddenly the fare beside him barked "Stick 'em up!" and without any warning fired a handgun pointblank at Midwinter.

Only a few minutes later, oilworker T. Hetherington was driving from the city to his work at a Calmont Oils wellsite in Turner Valley. An approaching coupe had slowed down, then sped past him towards Calgary. Someone in the coupe had yelled at him and pointed towards a field at the roadside. Hetherington quickly pulled off the road and got out of his car. As he made his way to the field he saw a man lying there, his hands and feet bound with wire. He was bleeding profusely from jagged wounds in his abdomen and was writhing in agony on the flattened grain. It was Ernest Midwinter, drenched in his own blood, still fully conscious.

Hetherington, not daring to move the wounded man by himself, flagged down other passing motorists, one of whom sped off for help. While they awaited the arrival of a Calgary ambulance, Midwinter managed to tell them something of what had happened. One of the quartet of thugs had shot him again while he struggled. Then they robbed him of the $15.50, bound him with fence wire, and dragged him into the field. Next, they piled into the taxi and took off, leaving Midwinter to perish. At the Holy Cross Hospital, before dying on the morning of 18 August, the second day after the shooting, he was able to give the APP a fair description of his assailants.

Armed with murder warrants for two of the men, the police began a massive search. They even hired aviator Fred McCall to do a low-level aerial search of the area. The taxi was spotted on a deadend trail east of DeWinton, presumably Dunbow Road, as it is known today.

It seems the thugs had abandoned the vehicle, then set off on foot in search of another getaway car. From there they apparently stole an old car and made their getaway to the United States. The car carried them into Montana, where it quit on them.

One-time High River resident John Edlund told me more about that end of the story. Edlund's father used to own and operate High River's Highwood Theatre, now the Wales, as well as the Valley Theatre in Turner Valley. In order to keep a close eye on both movie houses he commuted regularly between them.

John told me, "One August Sunday evening in 1930, when I was about twenty years old, Dad and I came out of the Highwood Theatre and he said, 'Son, did you use the car today?' I reminded him I didn't even drive a car, let alone use his. I remember it was quite a vehicle, a fine 1928 Oldsmobile. It had vanished. Dad seemed to recall some strange-looking guys eyeing it as he went to work in the Highwood Theatre earlier that evening."

Later that August week, the APP confirmed that

the four men who had taken the life of Ernest Midwinter has skulked on foot to High River and stolen the Olds from in front of the movie house. The press had reported that they had fled across the border in an "old car." "Old car, indeed!" John Edlund snorted to me. "Racing south to get away they burned out the bearings and blew the engine. The police found it down there and we just had to abandon it. Those guys were the kind to destroy everything."

In addition to the dying Midwinter's description of his attackers, the APP had one unusual clue. On the blood-soaked ground where Midwinter had been dumped, they found an odd-shaped wooden "billy." Its photograph was given to the press along with a notice that a reward was being offered for its identification. In no time an Edmonton garage mechanic came to the APP offices and admitted he had made the club for his own protection. It had recently been stolen, but he thought he knew the thief. That clue led the APP to begin looking for Albert E. Allen, an ex-Edmonton taxi driver now suspected of being the trigger man.

The "mounties in blue" learned that the four culprits had been seen in a little town near Chicago. There they had split up. Allen's trail led west to the state of Washington. The Alberta police, acting on a tip from local police, moved in on a patch of tangled brush beside a lake about two miles from the milk-canning town of Carnation, a short distance east of Seattle. There they pounced on Allen, who sat peacefully beside a cliff-side shelter, weaving baskets.

Meanwhile, fingerprint experts in Vancouver, Ottawa, and Washington led the APP to the prison at Leavenworth, Kansas, where J. Petrie had begun a three-year term for car theft. Petrie's real name was Mike Radko. He had a criminal record, was wanted in Saskatchewan and Alberta, and was being sought by the Saskatchewan mounted police. The APP knew they had the other man on the arrest warrant for the Midwinter murder. The third and fourth members of the quartet, it was discovered, had not been involved in the shooting. Police felt they would be nabbed eventually even though they had vanished into Chicago's warrenlike underworld.

Both of these murders, in those days when homicides were rare, revealed the same meritorious perseverance, ingenuity, and tenacity that distinguishes today's police services.

Waste Not, Want Not

LONG BEFORE RECYCLING BECAME A FASHIONable buzzword, we had such meaningful expressions as "make-do," "hand-me-down," and "adapted." By that we meant giving a product a second life, a renewed purpose, knowing it would likely be just as useful and, perhaps, even as attractive as it was the first time around.

In Depression years old flour bags were bleached and reused as pillow cases and underwear, strips of worn auto tires wound up as shoe resoles, a stripped-down car chassis was reincarnated as a "Bennett buggy."

Families and communities were proud of their ability to turn yesterday's worn-out, obsolete, or inadequate items to another use. Over the years, thanks to the ingenuity of civic staff workers in the offices and in the field, recycling has continued to be a common practice in Calgary.

Tons of sandstone chips were inevitably produced in the course of quarrying and carving building blocks for civic buildings and residences. It is still possible to see these sandstone walls in basements and above ground on a number of pioneer building sites. In 1956 the stately home of Senator Pat Burns on Fourth Street West was demolished to make way for the Colonel Belcher Hospital. Dozens of its sandstone blocks were trucked across town to be used for contouring and terracing the lovely Patrick Burns Memorial Rock Gardens on the Tenth Street NW hillside above Riley Park.

On Twelfth Avenue East the old unserviceable General Hospital, for many years the Isolation Hospital, was demolished. But part of its sandstone remains were repositioned and accented to become a ruinlike monument to this institution that sheltered early southern Alberta patients. In 1941 some other sandstone remains were rescued from neglect and vandalism and given a new purpose. Blocks were hauled from the site of an incomplete mansion that pioneer Dr. Neville Lindsay had been building for his wife on a sandy hillside overlooking the Elbow River. They were put to new use as gateposts at the entrance to St. Mary's Cemetery on the hilltop near the Union Cemetery.

Calgary went so far as to move entire buildings in order to prolong their usefulness and allow them to continue giving pleasure to our growing population. Two good examples, which were built as not-too-distant neighbours on Fourth Avenue West, now dwell in a type of retirement at Heritage Park. One of them is the Prince House, recycled in all its turn-of-the-century dignity, and nearby stands the sandstone bungalow that once was the home of Calgary's founder, Colonel James Macleod.

Heritage Park specializes in giving old-timers a recycled lifespan. Another such building is the log cabin occupied in 1882 by federal government surveyor Archie McVittie. When Eighth Avenue East was undergoing a facelift the cabin was moved to St. George's Island where it became a craft shop,

Calgary's most-photographed citizen, Dinny the Dinosaur, has some rather interesting innards. *Courtesy Glenbow-Alberta Institute/*NA-3884-13

then a first aid post of the St. John Ambulance Brigade.

A certain St. George's Island resident is an example of some rather bizarre recycling. In 1934 the Calgary Zoological Society hired Finnish-born John Kanerva to sculpt fifty-six reptilian monsters– this area's original inhabitants– for its new prehistoric park. A team of expert palaeontologists and the renowned Banff sculptor Charlie Biel assisted Kanerva in his efforts to make the creatures appear authentic. The largest of the life-sized replicas was a Brontosaurus that has turned out to be Calgary's most photographed citizen, Dinny the Dinosaur.

John Kanerva, his son Bill, and a crew of about six, took five weeks to build the enormous creature. They used steel rods and metal lath for the framework from which they fashioned the cement outer shell. Dinny stands 10.6 metres tall, is 39.6 metres in length, and weighs 109 tonnes. While watching the construction, zoo curator Tom Baines got an idea. In order to help the giant lizard replica withstand our climate and enjoy a long life, he had three obsolete comfort stations hauled over from where they sat on the trash heap, and dumped them into Dinny's almost completed belly. (If you don't know what a "comfort station" is I suggest you ask your grandparents.)

All Calgary administration economies were not as offbeat. Back about 1919 our rapidly expanding street railway system found itself burdened with seven rather inadequate little four-wheeled streetcars. Calgary Municipal Railway's superintendent, Thomas McCauley, heard that Saskatoon had a problem. Its transit network had six hefty eight-wheelers whose weight was more than the city's bridges could bear. So an out-and-out swap took place leaving everyone happy.

In 1935 a fire at the car barns alongside the exhibition grounds on Second Street East badly damaged five trams parked there between shifts. Using economical ingenuity, the street railway staff rebuilt four of the vehicles even though it meant turning one of them end-to-end to accomplish the task. In that car-barn shop the mechanics built a mad-looking tram using scrap metal for a frame, an old passenger car four-wheeled truck and trolley pole, and a driver's cabin of tongue-and-groove panelling. It functioned as a freight-hauler for years. Down on those same fairgrounds, now known as Stampede Park, the old city steam power plant had its electricity-making equipment removed and served as a chuckwagon storage barn for many more years.

Calgary's praiseworthy thriftiness extended to its bridges, too. The spidery iron Louise Bridge that took Tenth Street NW across the Bow River was trundled up the river valley to extend its usefulness in Ghost River country. One local iron span even changed rivers. First it linked Calgary's old townsite east of the Elbow with the new centre of the city. Then, replaced by a heavier Ninth Avenue East bridge in 1897, it was lugged over to the north shore of St. George's Island to carry traffic over the north channel of the Bow, until it was replaced by the Baines Bridge in 1964. An unusual recycling job involved an aluminium span, originally part of an overhead direction sign at the intersection of the Trans-Canada Highway and the Barlow Trail. It reappeared at the west end of Glenmore Lake as the substructure of a pedestrian bridge.

There are many examples of useful and decorative recycling throughout our city. A flag pole that once rose above the mounted police barracks at Fort Calgary found a new home in Riley Park in 1914. Royal Doulton gargoyles, saved from destruction when the beautiful Herald (later Greyhound)

Building was demolished to make way for the Len Werry hulk, were given high profile roles in various locations.

The elderly sandstone CPR railway depot also was destined for reincarnation around 1912. Hauled south on railway flat cars, the express and baggage section of the station was repositioned as the Claresholm railway depot. The waiting room and ticket office part, also constructed of Pincher Creek sandstone, moved to a new trackside location at High River where it now houses the town's museum.

Let nobody in today's throw-away society smugly tell you that recycling is a fine new idea. It was an essential endeavour in an older world plagued by impoverished circumstances when the words "Waste Not, Want Not" really meant something.

Making Do

THE FIRST WHITE ALBERTA HOMEMAKERS were a hardy bunch–by necessity rather than choice. Those who learned to cope with their new life did so largely on their own, for in those days there was a discouraging shortage of physical help and moral support.

Mrs. John McDougall recalled living in a tent after arriving at the Morley Mission in 1873. Later her missionary husband, with the help of local Indians, built their first house of logs. "We had neither boards nor shingles so the roof was of poles covered with sod to keep out the rain, while the floor was plain mother earth. The windows were made of parchment, and when we wanted to look outside we opened the door!"

Elizabeth McDougall's first storage cupboard was made from the sides of a packing case, with parchment paper for shelves. Apparently that was strong enough, for, as she said, "We had little to put on them." The table and chairs were homemade, as well, and the bedstead was of poles attached to the wall. "It was not until several years later that we had factory-made furniture."

Rancher Fred Ings recounted that the passage of time often softened memories of the hardships. He spoke of two pioneer women reminiscing of the "fun they used to have converting old packing cases and barrels–with the aid of muslin and chintz–into presentable dressing tables, of turning cheese boxes into chairs, and stuffing ticks with hay to make mattresses, and lacing rawhide to form bedsprings."

Isabella Christine, eldest daughter of Richard Hardisty, chief factor at Fort Resolution, spent her premarital days in what they called "the Big House," inside the fort. The furniture she remembered from childhood days had been built by hand by the resident Hudson's Bay carpenter. When she married James Lougheed, a young Calgary lawyer, the newlyweds moved into an empty two-room tailor shop on Stephen Avenue, then added a bay window (the first in the settlement), a kitchen, and a large bedroom.

As Calgary grew, the Lougheeds had the house moved by rolling it on logs to a more fashionable neighbourhood closer to the Bow River.

Though pioneer women were few in number, they made the most of opportunities for community activities. The Lougheeds were a popular host and hostess couple. "Those were the days of real western hospitality," recalled Lady Lougheed in later years. "Every New Year the men called at our homes from 9 A.M. until midnight, and sometimes we had as many as a hundred callers."

"Social life centred about the church, where concerts were given. I played the organ and my husband taught Sunday school," recalled Mrs. John Irwin, wife of a pioneer grocer. She came to Calgary as a young girl to keep house for her father, who had been here for two years by that time. He had built a two-storey frame house on the south bank of the Bow River at the foot of McTavish (Centre) Street where Chinatown is today. She attended nearby Central School and remembered being particularly proud of the family's pump organ. Her musical talent made her a favourite member of her church congregation.

One historic social function Mrs. Irwin remembered was the large picnic she and her father attended when the first sod was turned to mark the start of the Calgary-Edmonton Railway in 1890. Early Calgarian Ada Dowling, who became the wife of John R. Costigan, attended that same event. Ada's father was a mounted police inspector, and, before her marriage, she instructed primary grades at Sleepy Hollow School on Stephen Avenue East and taught music lessons to several Calgary youngsters.

Ada recalled the excitement of dressing up for social functions after she had married Costigan. She particularly remembered the annual Mounted Policemen's Ball. It took place at Boynton Hall across Stephen Avenue from her school, and was one of the year's social highlights.

Mrs. A.G. Woolley-Dod, who settled with her rancher husband south of Calgary in 1889, spoke of the neighbourhood camaraderie. "There used to be great coyote hunts then, as there were hardly any fences and plenty of prairie chickens. Several years after our arrival polo was started, the Pine Creek polo ground being a mile from our house. We saw many a good match there, and at the old polo grounds in Hillhurst. Polo Week at High River was, for many years, the most pleasant event of the summer . . . "

That precious comradeship was shared by a young woman who did not arrive from somewhere else. She was Lillian Costello, the first white girl born in Calgary, when the population stood at two hundred. Summing up the mood of the times she said, "We were all like one big family, and if parcels of good things to eat would come . . . they would all be shared by neighbours."

Foodstuffs, in fact, were additional proof that those pioneer women not only had strong backs and wills, they had rugged digestive systems. Mrs. David McDougall said, "Our food consisted mostly of meat, morning, noon, and night, until I could have cried for joy to have some of the fresh fruit from my old home in Ontario. The meat pot was always on the fire, forever cooking on the large box iron stove . . . "

Her sister-in-law had this to say: "Our living consisted mostly of wild meat, chickens, buffalo meat, and sometimes fish. We had neither fruit nor vegetables, getting potatoes once in two years and apples once in seven years."

An especially vivid memory for Mrs. David McDougall was the preparation of buffalo meat for the winter, a task accomplished by both the Indian and white women. The meat and marrow were boiled and poured into rawhide bags in batches weighing from five to twenty pounds. "As the bags cooled they were turned continuously so that the fat would be distributed equally throughout the pemmican. Large quantities of the meat were sun-dried, while the hard fat was saved for candle dips, the only light the settlement knew."

Isabel Drever, who became the bride of Colonel James Macleod of Fort Calgary fame, had a special memory of her first meal under cover, which happened to be Christmas dinner in 1876. The colonel had made a special trip to Helena, returning with a turkey, a dozen eggs, for which he had paid six dollars, and some raisins for the home-made plum pudding. "They made a fine holiday dinner!"

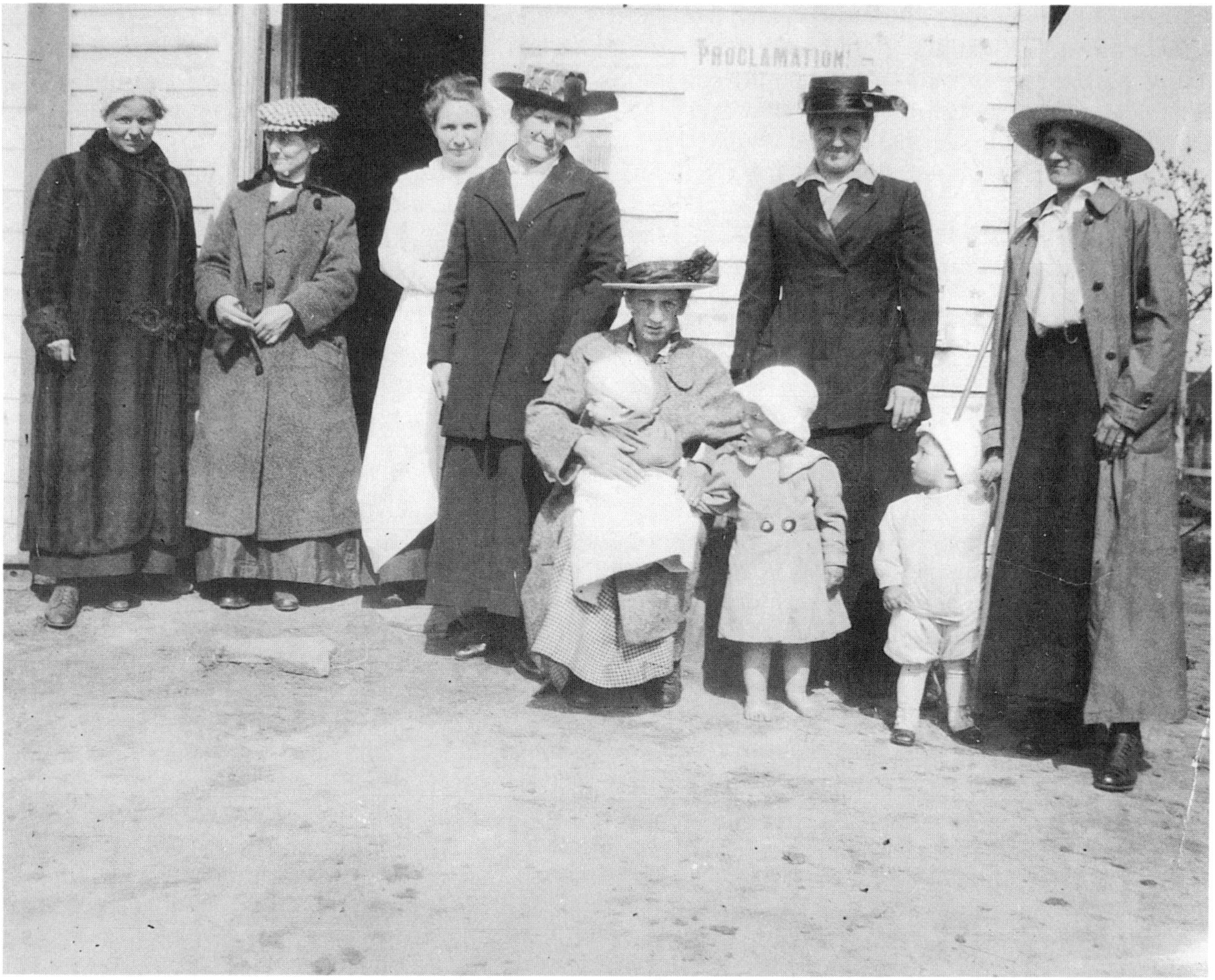

Early Calgary homemakers depended on one another for companionship and support as they made a life for their families on the frontier. *Courtesy Glenbow-Alberta Institute/NA-2163-3*

Understandably, a handful of the pioneer women lacked the stamina of body and spirit to survive the rigours and deprivations of the frontier. Certainly even the most fit and courageous did not thrive on the adversity of pioneer life. One of those hardy immigrant women who did stick it out on the frontier summarized it this way: "We spent so much time planning and contriving how to make things comfortable and keep our family clothed and fed that we didn't have time to worry about the things we didn't have." That, and the companionship of other women who found themselves in similar circumstances, helps explain the success of these early Calgary homemakers.

Merry (Christmas) Memories

CHRISTMAS AT OUR KILLARNEY HOUSE IN THE 1920s was always completely predictable, which is probably why the memories remain with me to this day. The same dear friends sat with us around the dinner table, the same jokes were told, the same toasts were proposed, and, when the table was cleared and the dishes washed and put away, the same old songs were sung around the grey Nordheimer upright piano in our living room.

Beginning about a month before Christmas, my sister, Mary, and I had special annual chores. One was taking turns stirring the heavy, gooey Christmas cake and plum pudding mixtures. There would be large puddings for Christmas and New Year's, and smaller ones for birthdays during the year. Each pudding was placed in a bowl of the proper size, and encased in a laced-up cloth. The Christmas pudding received regal treatment. With mock ceremony, we dropped tiny silver favours into its batter, among them a donkey, a love-knot, a ring, a heart, a nickel, and a horseshoe–each one signifying a measure of fortune in the coming year. We children received only a small ration of the hard white pudding sauce, Granny's "old secret recipe," for it was generously laced with brandy.

One immediate pre-Christmas chore for Mary and me was traipsing north across the gravelled road of Seventeenth Avenue West, up and across the sloping field to Tom Jackson's fir-tree-lined farm. There we would watch him choose, catch, and behead a turkey. Still warm, its outstretched wings bumping our legs, we would puff heavily as we carried it home. Then came the hateful job of plucking it. I, who had vague thoughts of becoming a doctor, was fascinated as Mother removed its innards, assigning some of them to a pot of boiling water where they became part of her famous giblet gravy and stuffing that always accompanied her traditional bread sauce.

As Christmas Day wore on, the kitchen grew hotter and more aromatic. Mary and I had the job of setting the table, which had completely filled the small dining room once all of its extensions were added. The silver, glassware, china, holly, poinsettias, placemats, crackers with paper hats inside, and dishes of nuts, raisins, and dates soon loaded the table, well before it was time to bring in the food.

Discipline on Christmas Day took the form of an early race to dress in my boy scout uniform, then, as Santa's emissary, to dole out gifts for the children at the Salvation Army Booth Memorial Home two blocks away. Next, a quick breakfast and our family was off to nearby St. Martin's church for the eleven o'clock service. Then, impatiently, we had a noontime snack before pouncing on the gaily wrapped treasures under the tree.

For days, Mother had been smuggling parcels that had arrived by mail into her bedroom closet

Jack and his sister, Mary, were an integral part of the Christmas preparations at the Peach residence. This photo of Jack and Mary on the roof of the Hudson's Bay store was taken ca. 1919. *Courtesy Glenbow-Alberta Institute/NA-1616-10*

before anyone could pry, prod, or rattle them. The gift-giving imagination of my maternal grandmother from England was boundless, and her parcel, which had travelled by sea and train, was always the most prized. It was never a large parcel, but into it she packed tiny, individually wrapped surprises for each of us. We were not allowed to open any of these until every bit of the package's waterproof wrapping was carefully removed and flattened, each knot untied in the network of string, every ribbon unknotted and folded. This dissecting of Granny's potpourri of love was an annual ritual of patience and discovery.

The guests trooped in about six o'clock, most having earned the appellation of "uncle" or "aunt" from long, close associations with the family in war and in peace, the men having been Father's bachelor chums before World War I. In no time, the meal would be demolished, the stories told, and the dishes done by Mary and me. After plenty of spirited conversation, storytelling, laughter, and carols, our guests would trail out into the night to catch the last streetcar back into the little city at the end of one more traditional Christmas at our home.

Index

About the Author

*B*ORN AND RAISED IN CALGARY, Jack Peach sold his first writing at the age of nine. He worked for more than forty-five years in radio and television while pursuing a writing career, which resulted in articles in magazines and journals throughout Canada and around the world. His appearances on the CBC and his regular columns in the *Calgary Herald* and the *Calgary Sun* provided hours of reading and listening enjoyment for his many fans. He was the author of several books, including the recent bestseller *Days Gone By*. He won numerous awards for his writing, including a City of Calgary Centennial Award of Merit in recognition of his "outstanding contribution to the enrichment of life in Calgary," and a certificate of recognition from the federal Ministry of Multiculturalism and Citizenship for his contribution to Canadian citizenship "as an historian, writer, broadcaster, and promoter of Canadian symbols and values."